CREATION AND GOSPEL

TORONTO STUDIES IN THEOLOGY

CREATION AND GOSPEL

THE NEW SITUATION IN EUROPEAN THEOLOGY

GUSTAF WINGREN

with introduction and bibliography by
Henry Vander Goot

THE EDWIN MELLEN PRESS
NEW YORK AND TORONTO

CREATION AND GOSPEL

THE NEW SITUATION IN EUROPEAN THEOLOGY

by

Gustaf Wingren

with an Introduction and a Bibliography

by

Henry Vander Goot

Copyright © 1979

by

The Edwin Mellen Press
Suite 918
225 West 34th Street
New York, New York 10001

Library of Congress Cataloging Number 78-78183

ISBN 0-88946-994-6

Printed in the United States of America

Creare est semper novum facere.

Creation is continuously to make new.

Martin Luther

PREFACE

These lectures were prepared by Professor Gustaf Wingren for his North American tour in January and February, 1979. In our invitation, we requested that he introduce his basic theological ideas and program without presuming specific knowledge of contemporary Swedish theology on the part of his audience. It is characteristic of North American theology today not to be conversant with ongoing work in Europe. Moreover, theologians working north of the German theological colossus tend to be especially overlooked, a fact that we Canadians, living north of the American colossus, can well understand.

Yet it is precisely from such boundary areas that new orientations and fruitful criticisms of dominant tendencies frequently arise. Swedenborg, Kierkegaard, and Nygren are Scandinavians who have profoundly affected North American theology. Gustaf Wingren, with his "Creation Faith," continues this great tradition, both renewing the classical creation faith for us and presenting a passionate critique of contemporary European theology. He also discusses social and political factors affecting the European church and theological education today, introducing us along the way to some Scandinavian thinkers who are not well known in North America, e.g., K. Løgstrup and Ole Jensen.

For various reasons which Professor Wingren himself has given, he has not yet found a specific denominational audience in North America. There is no large church

here which would claim him as typically "its own."
This is because Wingren unites so many different tendencies in his work. Though a Lutheran, he is Swedish
and hence more Catholic than most North American Lutherans. His theological inspiration comes more from Irenaeus than from Luther and hence he interprets salvation
as renewal and recapitulation of creation, what some
might call a "Calvinist motif." He is, in addition, more
oriented to the German theological debate (Barth, Bultmann, Moltmann) than most Swedish theologians. For all
these reasons, Professor Wingren is an original and
seminal thinker who offers new possibilities for our
own constructive endeavors.

Two things about Professor Wingren's lectures
strike me as particularly valuable. First, his argument that the present situation of the church is closer
to the third century than to any later time, and that the
law-gospel distinction might today be restated in analogy with Irenaeus' death-resurrection distinction, seems an
especially fruitful suggestion. It offers us a new
perspective on certain ecclesiastical and theological
problems that are urgent for us all.

Second, Professor Wingren's "Theology of Creation-
Faith" offers a new foundation for contemporary Christian ethics, a third alternative to the either/or of
"natural law" or "Christocentism." It will be interesting to see how his proposals are developed and applied by his North American colleagues in ethics. That
his work has already elicited enthusiastic response
here in certain quarters is evidenced by his present
North American tour.

In any undertaking of this kind, so many persons
and institutions are involved that it is impossible to

give recognition to each one. Therefore, I proffer this
acknowledgement and general thanksgiving. Yet three persons should be singled out because of their initiating
and organizing Professor Wingren's visit: Henry Vander
Goot of Calvin College, Herbert Richardson of the University of St. Michael's College, and James Olthuis of
the Institute for Christian Studies. I am also grateful
to Mrs. Una Crist for typing and preparing this volume
during these twelve days of Christmas, 1978.

   Finally, most to be thanked are Professor Wingren
and his wife, who is accompanying him throughout this
tour. That they have favoured us with their presence
and with this present volume of lectures is a gift which
we gladly receive. On behalf of my many colleagues, I
say "Welcome. We rejoice to have you be among us."

                              Douglas Jay
                              Toronto School of Theology
                              Epiphany, 1979

CONTENTS

INTRODUCTION

HENRY VANDER GOOT

Gustaf Wingren is Sweden's most notable contemporary theologian. The son of working parents of the middle class, Wingren was born on November 29, 1910 in a small manufacturing town in western Sweden. His contact with the local Swedish Lutheran Church there was by no means unusual. Wingren has frequently mentioned his own early childhood experiences of the church's irrelevance to the basic issues of life in the everyday world, and he has done this in an effort to shed light on his own work and choice of theological topics.[1]

Wingren's student years were spent largely in Lund. In 1929 Wingren graduated from the private elementary schools there and in the fall of the same year became a student at the University of Lund. Theology and philosophy were his "college" areas of specialization. In the fall of 1935 Wingren became a candidate in the faculty of theology, and in the fall of 1939 he completed his licentiate degree in dogmatics and symbolics by submitting a thesis on Irenaeus and Marcion.[2] The great German historian, Friedrich Loofs, was the then-acclaimed Irenaeus authority. Furthermore, Adolf von Harnack had reconstructed a Marcion corpus from fragments. Hence, Wingren felt that a doctoral dissertation on either Irenaeus or Marcion would be impossible to execute at Lund. Especially in the case of Marcion, no thesis could be defended because adequate tools and materials with which to criticize Harnack's work were not available.

However, since Wingren was surrounded at Lund by
eminent Luther experts, he was encouraged to write a
doctoral dissertation in the area of Luther research.
Wingren has mentioned in particular Herbert Olsson as a
most important influence in these years.[3] Hence, in the
spring of 1942, Wingren submitted to the theological
faculty at Lund a dissertation on Luther's idea of vocation and successfully defended it shortly thereafter.[4]
In the fall, 1942, Wingren was appointed *docent* in systematic theology and remained an assistant in the theological faculty until 1951.

In the meanwhile, however, Wingren lectured extensively elsewhere, in and outside of Sweden. Especially
noteworthy was a 1947 semester in Basel, during which
time he replaced Karl Barth. Upon Wingren's return to
Lund a vacancy was created in the department of systematic theology by the retirement (from the chair of theological ethics) of the famous Anders Nygren, who was about
to assume his duties as the new Bishop of Lund. For nearly three years a search was conducted to fill this prestig-
ious post. Finally, in May of 1951, Nygren hesitantly
concurred that the appointment be extended to Wingren.
The inaugural ceremonies took place on November 3, 1951,
at which time Wingren was elevated to one of the only two
professorships of systematic theology available at state
universities in the entire country. Wingren thus attained
to one of the most important posts in Swedish Lutheran
state-church culture and life. From this post he was
emeritated in 1977.

Frequently lecturing at major European university
centers (Oslo, Uppsala, Kiel, Birmingham, Cambridge, Freiburg, Göttingen, Tübingen), Wingren has received the honorary doctorate from the University of Kiel in 1965, St.

Andrews in 1966, Rostock (DDR) in 1969 and Aarhus (Denmark) in 1978. Wingren has also become very active in the Lutheran World Federation and in the Ecumenical Movement. In the Ecumenical Movement he has become especially noted for his work on the International Faith and Order Commission.

As in the lives of most of us, main orientations are established in the early years. This is surely true of Gustaf Wingren and the development of his theology of creation. The major circumstances accounting to a large extent for the character, content and tone of Wingren's production were present prior to 1960. After this time only their full impact and significance has come to more complete and explicit manifestation. Six circumstances in particular are of major importance. These are (1) Wingren's relationship to Swedish, especially the so called "Lundensian," theology; (2) Wingren's early contact with European Neo-orthodoxy; (3) Wingren's dependence upon the Danish Protestant Lutheran philosophy of Knut Løgstrup of Aarhus; (4) Wingren's relation to ecclesiastical developments in Sweden, especially to high-church Lutheranism; (5) Wingren's vocation as a theological ethicist; and (6) Wingren's extensive work in the ecumenical movement. In introducing Gustaf Wingren to the reader, I have chosen to focus only on the first three of these, since I judge them to be the most significant.

1.   Wingren and the Lundensian "School"

As a theological student at Lund, Wingren quite naturally came to work in the manner of the so called Lundensian theology. Moreover, the Lundensian theology represents the context in which Wingren's special stress on creation first appeared. A brief description of this theology and "School" is thus in order here.

The Lundensian "School" revolved around three major
figures: Gustaf Aulén, Anders Nygren, and Ragnar Bring.
Aulén had been a pupil of Nathan Söderblom and a close
friend of Einar Billing, two famous scholars at the University of Uppsala. In 1913 Aulén became professor of
systematic theology at the University of Lund. In 1924
Anders Nygren became professor of theological ethics
there. In 1929, Ragnar Bring finished his doctoral dissertation and was quickly appointed *docent* under Aulén.
During his absence from Lund (until 1934, when he returned
to succeed Aulén in the chair of dogmatics), Bring concentrated on philosophical questions concerning method in
theology. His study involved critical argumentation and
the collaboration of Nygren. Bring's conclusion was that
theology is essentially an historical discipline.

To all three theologians (Aulén, Nygren, and Bring)
it had become increasingly clear that all science (including theology, if it aspires to be scientific at all)
is bound to the experiential horizon (Kant), and that this
horizon reveals the ineradicable and irreducible presence
of universal religious experience (Schleiermacher). Scientific theology is not concerned with God, or with the experience of transcendence as such; rather it deals with
the various concrete and historical ways in which the
"eternal" is given symbolization in the spiritual life of
man and society. Any violation of these presuppositions
of thought causes theology to lose its *scientific* character.

The object of theological science is thus the religions, each of which is individual and unique. According
to the Lundensian School, the historical religions all
stand alongside one another, each representing a concrete,
historical, instance of the finite experience of the
"eternal." How these actual occurrences of religion

differ from one another determines what they are. In a
typically historicist fashion, the Lundensian School
identifies each religion by what differentiates it from
the others. To scientific theology is left the task of
characterization and description. Theology circumscribes
the religions according to their concrete historical individuality.

Furthermore, according to the Lundensians, each
religion is governed by a basic motif, a recurrent, sal-
ient, thematic element that provides the tradition with
its unity, wholeness, and distinctiveness. Systematic
theology is the effort to research motifs, and to determine the compatibility of the materials circumscribed by
each religion with this core concept or structural center.

According to Lundensian theology, three major religious traditions have dominated Western European history:
Christianity, Judaism, and Hellenism. Their fundamental
motifs are *Agape, Nomos,* and *Eros,* respectively. It is
this specific typology of Western religions and the philosophical and theological position upon which it rests
that Aulén, Nygren, and Bring contribute to the constitu-
tion of the Lundensian tradition in theology.

According to Wingren himself, it was in the early
thirties that many began to speak expressly about a Lundensian "School" of thought.[5] In 1930 Aulén published his
famous *Christus Victor,*[6] the same year as Part I of Nygren's *Agape* and *Eros;*[7] and in 1933 Bring published *Till
frågan om den systematiska teologiens uppgift* (literally:
"On the Question of the Task of Systematic Theology").[8]
Though the biblical school of Uppsala regarded the theologians of Lund as under the influence of Continental,
dialectical theology (Christianity = *Agape*), the Continental theologians themselves disavowed the association.
Lundensian theology was philosophically based on neo-

Kantian philosophy. Furthermore, its theological method
was strictly historical. Both of these factors formed a
sharp contrast to prevailing attitudes on the Continent.[9]

Presupposing that theological work is essentially
historical research, the Lundensian School assigned to
Christian systematic theology the task of an historical
investigation of the Christian tradition. The essence of
that tradition and the New Testament ideal—the specifically Christian vis-á-vis *Nomos* and *Eros* piety—was desig-
nated the "*Agape* motif."

The appearance of the *Agape* motif outside of the
New Testament was alleged to occur most strikingly in the
theologies of Marcion, Irenaeus, and Luther. Hence, in
good Lundensian style, Wingren very early occupied himself
with the theology of Marcion,[10] moving from there quite
quickly to Irenaeus.[11] Wingren's unpublished licentiate
thesis was a comparative study of the ideas of creation
and law in the theologies of Marcion and Irenaeus.

In a recent article, Wingren says that he can give
no reason for this selection of creation and law as topics
in his early studies: "I do not know why my interests were
from the very beginning of my theological studies directed
to the idea of creation and the first article of the Creed;
this is just simply the way it was."[12] Elsewhere, however,
Wingren does seem to shed some light on this matter. Describing his personal experience before becoming a student
of theology, Wingren says: "I have always sought to choose
topics that throw light on the integrating function of the
Christian faith in human life as a whole."[13]

Indeed, one of the chief concerns that typifies Wingren's entire theological program in the desire to display
the content of the Christian faith in a manner meaningful
and applicable to the lives of men in the everyday world.
It has been Wingren's lifelong conviction—clearly express-

ing his stress on creation and law—that "it is a hope-
less task to achieve an attitude of faith towards existence just when the Word reaches man, if up to that moment
each earthly event is regarded as unrelated to God.[14] In
fact, his desire to demonstrate how preaching (the Word
in Scripture) links up with existence explains Wingren's
frequent theological emphasis on a "double phenomenological orientation" in theology.[15]

This deep-seated conviction that theology's problem
today is essentially a hermeneutical one appears especially in *The Living Word* (1949). Wingren has described his
concern as follows: "to combine the Word as 'kerygma' and
the outside as 'creation.'"[16] In *The Living Word,* Wingren
tries to articulate the unity underlying the duality of
creation and preaching, of the world "out there" and the
Word as spoken in the congregation, or of law and gospel.
Says Wingren:

> Just as it can be said of our preaching today that
> it does not deal with real sin, nor expose the
> agony caused by death, but with an odd "good will"
> glosses over the thralldom of man, so it can also
> be said that the real consciousness of sin in the
> depths of the soul, on the one side, and the procla-
> mation of the Church, on the other, do not meet each
> other today. It is a paradoxical situation that the
> forgiveness of sins is being declared continually in
> all our cities and villages and that, at the same
> time, year after year in the very places where that
> is the case scores of people are to be found who are
> tormented by unforgiven sin and cannot find a way
> out of their torment. Oftener than one imagines,
> these guilt-burdened people listen to the words of
> our preaching and absolution without the thought of
> God's forgiveness of their sins crossing their minds
> for a moment. Something must surely be lacking in
> the preaching when people experience this inability
> to hear. Proclamation itself must, in this case,
> be of such a nature that the hearers do not link up
> the realities in question with the life of every
> day—not, that is to say, with the ordinary life of
> the world but rather with that so-called "religious"
> life which is really nothing at all but a pure

> fiction, the Emperor's new clothes. Needed here,
> as in the story, is a real child who can cry aloud
> that a "religious" relationship cut off from all
> earthly relationships is nothing at all. So that
> we might not succeed in worming our way into such
> a realm, which in any case we could not reach,
> Christ became *man* and forgave whoredom, theft, em-
> bezzlement, fraud, etc.—not only forgave them,
> indeed, but took them on himself, lived amongst
> sinners and died as a thief.[17]

Yet, as Thor Hall has observed, it is exactly this
concern with the question of the meaning of the Word in
Scripture for the contemporary situation of man that is
absent from the Lundensian theology. Remarks Hall:

> There is a roadblock in the way of Bring's pro-
> gress in the faith-reflection field. In this
> situation, he is forced to look for another way
> to do theology, and he finds it: Instead of...
> presenting a thorough reinterpretation of the
> meaning of Christian faith in a contemporary
> linguistic framework, Bring turns to the history
> of faith, to the study of the doctrinal intentions
> of the best theologians of the past. Besides being
> a scientifically respectable endeavor, this his-
> torical-systematic motif-research gives the theo-
> logian a certain understanding of the essential
> motifs of Christian faith. A personal and con-
> temporary and constructive understanding of the
> meaning of the faith it is not, of course.[18]

During the years of his formal training in the Lundensian School, Gustaf Wingren also became painfully aware
of this historicist obliviousness to the centrality of the
hermeneutical question. In his encounter with Lundensian
theology, which stressed science and especially historical
research, Wingren became convinced that there was little
help to be found for the church in this tradition. Thus
Wingren regards the influence of the Lundensian School on
the church of Sweden as having had a conservative effect.
Moreover the eclipse since the '30s of the importance of
the Lundensian theology represents to Wingren a "emanci-
pation of the life of the church from Swedish academic
theology and its almost exclusive focus on the historical

task."[19]   The Lundensians seemed uninterested in faith-
reflection and the hermeneutical problem.

However, even on the level of a purely descriptive
analysis of the historical sources, Wingren regards the
Lundensian School as representing a deficient perspective.
Motif research and the analysis of *Agape* pass by the elements of creation and law in the investigation of historical texts. Wingren's suspicion is that this deficiency
is not related just to the Lundensian lack of concern
over the hermeneutical problem, but is also necessitated
by the intrinsic philosophical and theological presupoosi-
tions of motif research.

It was during the 1930s that Wingren began to become
aware of the theological and philosophical presuppositions
necessitating the identification of *Agape* as the fundamental motif of the Christian faith. Especially under the
influence of the Lundensian ethicist and Luther expert,
Herbert Olsson, whose book *Schöpfung, Vernunft und Gesetz
in Luthers Theologie* has left a marked impression on Wingren's entire thought, Wingren came to see especially the
ethical implications of *Agape* thought. In *Agape* theology
there is a strong tendency to derive a Christian ethic
from the New Testament concept of love, i.e. from the gospel. Commenting on the experience of the 1930s, especially on the theological challenge posed by the rise of German National Socialism, and drawing on his own discovery
of a new Luther and a new Irenaeus, whose views on creation and law tended to invalidate the adequacy of the
Agape motif as applied to them by the Lundensians, Wingren
says: "We [Olsson and his students] all saw the same historical realities, the role of belief in creation, the
doctrine of the law, etc. An ethic derived from the gospel was theologically impossible for us."[20]

By the mid-1930s Wingren had begun to feel ill-

disposed to Lundensian theology in general and uncomfort-
able with the method of motif research in particular. He
felt that the motif-method makes the historian alert only
to certain dimensions of the historical material. What
the method cannot handle drops out of focus when a characterization of the theology under consideration is made
according to the Lundensian typology of motifs. A certain
closedness to the historical material is thus created.

The realization, furthermore, that historical motif
research misses essential dimensions of the theologies of
Luther and of Irenaeus underlies Wingren's *Luther on Vocation* of 1942 and Wingren's *Man and the Incarnation: A
Study In the Biblical Theology of Irenaeus* of 1947. In
Luther on Vocation Wingren's primary concern is Luther's
doctrine of the callings and stations in life. Moreover,
this doctrine, which Luther develops out of the Genesis
story of creation, is identified by Wingren with Luther's
doctrine of the law as the means by which God rules in
the earthly kingdom, and not only encourages but finally
even coerces men under sin to render loving service to
God through the neighbor, thus fulfilling the purpose of
creation. In addition, in *Man and the Incarnation* Wingren's concern is Irenaeus' doctrine of recapitulation,
which is Irenaeus' view of the relationship of creation
and redemption. Redemption is not seen, according to
Wingren, as *new* creation, but primarily as the restoration of the integrity of the original creation. Moreover,
the Irenaean theme of "divinization" must not be understood,
according to Wingren, to imply metaphysical increase
through salvation to a transnatural and transhuman ultimate destiny. Rather it must be understood ethically as
the coincidence of God's command and purpose for mankind
with mankind's own will and purpose for itself.

Now it is specifically the positive correlation of

the duality of creation and recapitulation in Irenaeus and
the positive correlation of the duality of law and gospel in Luther that is violated, according to Wingren, by
placing Irenaeus and Luther under the *single*, general
historical and soteriological motif of *Agape*. Speaking
about his 1954 book *Theology in Conflict* and its relation to the two earlier historical studies on Luther and
Irenaeus, Wingren says:

> What is new about this study *Theology in Conflict*
> is that I have abandoned the ground motif concep-
> tion and no longer believe in motif research as a
> theological method. But this new factor rests upon
> two purely historical works, *Luther on Vocation*
> (1942) and *Man and the Incarnation: A Study In the
> Biblical Theology of Irenaeus* (1947), in which I
> very simply go to the historical material on crea-
> tion and law and gospel. I chose to go to the two
> sources where, according to Nygren, the *Agape* motif
> is most clearly present and I discovered that the
> views of Luther and Irenaeus cannot be adequately
> reproduced using the tools of motif research....I
> was nothing more than a student in the Lundensian
> school, but as a student I set myself the task of
> reading two great authors who represent the *Agape*
> motif. When I finished I knew a great deal more
> about Luther and Irenaeus than before, but in the
> process I was forced to abandon the whole apparatus
> of motif research because it did not jibe with the
> historical material.[21]

Thus by 1947 Wingren had broken with the Lundensian
method of theology as historical motif research. As this
break came more and more to the fore, Wingren also became
acutely aware of the constructive and *systematic* theological deficiencies of the Lundensian approach.

As a student in Lund, Wingren had inherited, however, a certain preoccupation with specific historical
sources in the Christian tradition. It is exactly the
constructive, theological perspectives represented by
these sources (Irenaeus and Luther) that would soon lead
Wingren to a constructive position of his own. This is

the most significant influence of the Lundensian theology
on Wingren: it left him with the sources from which he
would derive his own theological position. As Wingren
himself remarks:

> My connection with motif research does not express
> itself, first of all, in what I have said in the
> course of the years. If this were anyone's point
> of orientation, he would only discover a widening
> gulf between my position and motif research. Rather,
> my real connection with motif research, a connection
> that is unintentional, expresses itself first of all
> in *what material I have chosen for historical re-
> search.*[22]

2. The Contact with Karl Barth

After the publication of Man and the Incarnation
(1947), Wingren spent one semester at Basel filling in for
Karl Barth. Wingren sensed his own inadequacy. He had no
real constructive theological position of his own. He
lectured on historical material (Irenaeus and Luther), but
the students in Basel were interested only in biblical theology.[23] "What does the Bible have to say to us now?" was
the question of ultimate concern. There was little interest in historical research as such, other than to determine
the meaning of the Word of God for today. Contrary to the
prevailing emphasis in Sweden, the hermeneutical question
of biblical interpretation was considered primary at Basel.

It was at Basel that Wingren came to see this attitude as an alternative to the Lundensian idea of theology
as an historical discipline. Says Wingren:

> I could not find any objective reason for rejecting
> the young Barthians' attitude towards the question
> [of the meaning of the Scriptures as the Word now
> being preached], nor have I been able to find one....
> This became obvious to me in Basel in the summer of
> 1947. It was not the students' attitude toward the
> question that was at fault but my theological educa-
> tion. I had to admit this to myself when time and
> again I left my seminars on Wednesday evenings
> feeling spiritually shaken.[24]

Wingren agreed with Barth that the purpose of theology
is investigation of Scripture (or investigation of the
interpretation of Scripture). Theology is the attempt
to uncover not just what once was believed but what must
be believed now and how we must live today.

By the end of 1947 Wingren was back in Lund. By
this time he had the ingredients he needed to make a
systematic theological statement of his own. Hence he
turned from historical research to constructive theology.
He had given up the theological procedure of motif research and in his view saved both Luther and Irenaeus,
especially their theologies of creation and law, from
the injustice done them by this method. As with Barth,
the primary question for Wingren became the meaning of
the Word as a living Word for today.[25]

In 1948, attempting to state the meaning of the
Word, Wingren drew upon the very two historical sources
he had studied in breaking with the method of motif
analysis, namely Luther and Irenaeus. He attached himself sympathetically to these sources and understood them
differently than the forgers of the method of motif research. Thus in *The Living Word* Wingren created the first
statement of his theological position on the meaning of
the Word as a living Word for today.

But in so doing Wingren attached himself to a theological perspective on the Word that not only came into
conflict with the presuppositions of motif research but
with the Barthian theology as well. He agreed with Barth
(against Liberalism) on the "formal" question of the primacy of the Word as kerygma. But it was in Wingren's attachment to the ideas of creation and law in Irenaeus and
Luther that he came to see the inadequacy of Barthianism
on the "material" question of the meaning of the Word as
a living Word for today. Especially the attempt to focus

theology through Christology is seen by Wingren as a
threat to the Christian confession concerning God, the
Father Almighty, Maker of Heaven and Earth.

Referring to his abstract agreement with Barth on
the "formal" question of the fundamental nature of the
interpretation of Scripture as direct address—as the
Word now preached—Wingren remarks:

> But this was only one side of the matter. The
> other side was an equally clear understanding of
> Barth's failings. This understanding had to do
> with the content of what Barth maintained was the
> essence of the Bible, the incarnation. The modern
> negation of the belief in creation has Karl Barth
> as its spiritual father; all others are secondary
> and have grown up in his shadow. What I had been
> searching for in Luther, in Irenaeus, was of
> course a biblical truth too. But it was a bibli-
> cal truth denied by Barth.[26]

Wingren agreed with Barth that the question of theology
is the question of the meaning of the Word for today.
But once the content of the Word was specified according
to law and gospel in that order—which is an issue of concrete and therefore primary importance—the paths of
Barth and Wingren diverged markedly.[27]

As I have reported, Wingren in 1948 set himself the
task of combining the theology of creation (as gleaned
from his reinterpretation of Irenaeus and Luther) with
Scripture as preaching or kerygma. As Wingren has himself said, "The task before which I stood in 1948 was the
following: to combine the doctrine of creation with a view
of the Word of Scripture as *direct address, kerygma,
preaching*."[28] The result of Wingren's efforts is *The
Living Word*. In *The Living Word* Wingren makes his first
systematic theological statement. At the same time, he
lays the foundations for his subsequent work in critical
and constructive theology over the next twenty-five years.
Wingren's conviction is that the meaning of the Word as a

preached Word cannot be disclosed when viewed (in the
situation of impartial analysis) as supporting fundamental motifs and when described simply according to the
Agape concept.

According to Wingren, the New Testament presupposes
and forms a unity with the Old; gospel and restoration
presuppose—historically and theologically—creation and
law, or contact with God prior to the proclamation of the
gospel. Wingren's principle of the fundamental nature of
creation and law thus constitutes the constructive and
critical principle of *The Living Word*. Furthermore, it
is the fulcrum of all of the critical and systematic studies that flow directly from *The Living Word*, studies that
each develop one of the many dimensions of this most decisive of all of Wingren's works.

In suggesting that Wingren's later works (including the
open coming to terms with Nygren) flow directly from *The
Living Word,* I do not, however, wish to leave the impression that Wingren had already conceived or outlined his
systematics as a whole at the time he wrote this work. One
might legitimately question whether even the idea that a
developed and rounded systematic theology had been begun
and would involve several later studies was present in
1949. Certainly by 1949 the ground plan of *Theology in
Conflict* had already been present for nearly two years.
By then, Wingren had worked with Nygren and Barth but not
yet with Bultmann.

Describing in 1974 his task as he saw it in 1948,
Wingren admits that the basic building blocks of *Theology
in Conflict* (the so-called "dual phenomenological starting
point of preaching and law," or the "dual criterion of
'anthropological' and 'hermeneutical' assumptions") had
then already been discovered.[29] However, the project
could not then be executed, Wingren continues, because "a

principal, systematic work wholly devoted to the problem
of preaching had first to be introduced as a basis for
Theology in Conflict."[30]   Only against the background of
an explicitly articulated point of view of his own would the
open coming to terms with modern theology in general and
with Nygren in particular that he envisioned already in
1948 be possible.

Hence, though *Theology in Conflict* (the open attack
on Nygren) was the point towards which Wingren intended
to move in the late forties, the project of *The Living
Word* had first to be finished. Accordingly, it was inevitable that Wingren's plan for *Theology in Conflict*
(which includes the attack on Nygren) would play a noticeable role in *The Living Word* itself, for it was only in
contrast to other perspectives, particularly that of Nygren's motif analysis, that the genuine achievement and
principle of *The Living Word* could be brought into proper
relief.

It is my judgment, then, that the exact sense and
content of Wingren's stress on the priority of creation
and law emerged first in the conflict with the perspective
of the Lundensian School in general and with Nygren's system in particular. Consequently, it is Wingren's conflict
with Lundensian theology that is the single most important
factor explaining the methodological and theological primacy of creation in the theology of Gustaf Wingren.

The key point in the conflict with Nygren is that
Nygren's method, which is essentially historical motif
analysis, neglects that aspect of the theological content
of historical materials having to do with creation and law.
Furthermore, the reason for this neglect is that intrinsic
philosophical assumptions cause Lundensian Theology to
subsume the Christian sources under the single organizing
notion of *Agape,* which is interpreted on alleged formal

grounds to be the essence of the New Testament and, therefore, the Christian ideal.

But we must speak of two phases in Wingren's break with Lundensian theology. In the *corpus* of Wingren there is material that only implicitly undermines the Lundensian method of motif research. This period is represented by Wingren's first two historical studies and by his abandonment of historical method in systematic theology in *The Living Word*. *The Living Word* also represents Wingren's entire theological program *in weltanschaulicher Form*. It is the platform from which Wingren chooses to speak in the growing rift with the philosophy and theology of Anders Nygren.

The second phase begins in 1951 when Wingren was appointed to succeed Nygren in the chair of theological ethics at the University of Lund. Certainly it is not inaccurate to say that the appointment was extended to Wingren in spite of *The Living Word,* which many observers apparently regarded as only a temporary derailment. However, even in Wingren's inaugural address it becomes clear that the Lundensian theology of Nygren has become for him a phenomenon to be observed as opposed to a position in which to stand and from which to speak. Throughout the lecture, Wingren stresses the dependence of Nygren's method of motif research on a concrete and specific philosophy of life, namely the critical Transcendentalism of the neo-Kantian philosophy of religion.[31] The groundwork for Wingren's open assault on Nygren had already been laid in *The Living Word*. However, the open attack itself can be regarded as beginning with Wingren's inaugural lecture when he was promoted (as Nygren's successor) to the chair of theological ethics at Lund. Its first systematic and comprehensive expression was achieved in 1954 in *Theology in Conflict*. However, after the ap-

pearance of *Theology in Conflict* an intense theological
and personal confrontation with Nygren took place. It
was this encounter that gave Wingren occasion to develop
further, and to lend precision to his critique of Nygren's system.

On February 7, 1956 Nygren was invited by the local
Theological Society (föreningen) at the University of
Lund to respond to *Theology in Conflict*. Nygren's comments were subsequently published in *Svensk Teologisk
Kvartalskrift*.[32] On the same evening Wingren was also
invited by the group to present a statement of his own
summarizing the points of tension between his own theology and the system of Nygren. This contribution to the
debate can also be found in *STK*.[33] A further elaboration
of his perspective on Nygren, together with an initial
response to Nygren's remarks of February 7, 1956, appears
later in *STK* under the title "Nomos och agape hos biskop
Nygren."[34]

It was to this last cited article that Nygren responded at great length in a subsequent article entitled
"Ytterligare till teologiens metodfråga."[35] By the time
Nygren's response had been published, tensions were clearly beginning to mount. (It is not unfair to say that the
reader of this debate as published in *STK*, must often
brush aside a surfeit of invective language and *argumenta
ad hominem* to penetrate to the core of the matter.) Wingren's final contribution fo the discussion represents
the major thrust of his response to Nygren's review of
Theology in Conflict. In this article entitled "Filosofi
och teologi hos biskop Nygren,"[36] Wingren develops as far
as he ever does the major questions raised in the debate.
Finally, this and Nygren's closing remarks[37] express
throughout a mutual feeling of frustration between the
two debaters that comes to a head in a bilateral refusal

to continue further discussion.

3. The Influence of Knut Løgstrup on Gustaf Wingren

The Wingren-Nygren altercation and the influence of Barth is an indispensible backdrop to a proper assessment of Wingren's subsequent attraction to the philosophy of Knut Løgstrup of Aarhus, Denmark. Yet this is not a sufficient background since it leaves open the question of Wingren's view of the relationship of philosophy and theology. Consequently, before we can turn directly to Løgstrup, we must review the development of Wingren's thinking on this question.

As we have already seen, Wingren rejected Nygren's grounding of theology in neo-Kantian philosophy. More recently he has interpreted Nygren's Logical Positivist modification of neo-Kantianism á la Axel Hägerström[38] as similarly deficient and as bound to a nineteenth century fact-value scheme.[39] Moreover, Bultmann's appropriation of the dialectic existentialism of Kierkegaard and Heidegger is rejected because, according to Wingren, it leads to the eclipsing of the biblical view of law and guilt.[40] Where, then, does Wingren stand on the relationship of philosophy to theology?

Given this background, it is not surprising that Wingren's position that Scripture must be allowed to interpret itself and that every attempt to permit an alien discipline to decree the content of theology has been interpreted by many in a Barthian sense, that is, as a rejection of philosophy as such. For example, Thor Hall has accused Wingren of reverting to a radically kerygmatic and therefore anti-philosophical stance.[41] Hall acknowledges no important differences between the position of · Wingren and the view of Barth. But this view of Wingren's position will not stand under closer scrutiny.

Wingren's view of the relationship between theology
and philosophy cannot be understood within the context of
the Nygrenian-Barthian alternative. To place Wingren on
the question of philosophical method in theology within
these alternatives is too simplistic. Moreover, such a
view ignores crucial material in the Wingren *corpus*. Wingren's position is neither a Nygrenian approach of grounding revelationally based theology in a non-revelationally
based philosophy, nor is it a Barthian approach oriented
to revelationally grounded theology alone which is then
itself thought adequate to furnish both content and onto-
logical ground. According to Wingren, both approaches are
inadequate. Both lead to the eclipse of creation and the
universal element of the law.

To adequately understand Wingren's view of what the
consequences of attachment to prevailing philosophies has
meant for theology, we must understand what Wingren has
judged the intrinsic philosophic matter to be that has
prevented Lundensian theology in particular, and other
philosophies in general, from adequately grasping Christianity's historical sources. In this way we can clarify
Wingren's position on the relationship of philosophy and
theology—and as well Wingren's attraction to Løgstrup's
thought.

As we noted above, Wingren rejects the motif research methodology of Lundensian theology because it is
not adequate to the historical material as such. Moreover, Wingren has concluded from this that intrinsic
philosophic matters are to blame and that therefore "the
historical materials in effect force a revision of the
Lundensian method in theology."[42] What is that intrinsic
philosophic matter that Wingren has thought it necessary
to challenge?

According to Wingren, Nygren's theological method of historical motif research is closely tied to neo-Kantian philosophy. According to neo-Kantian philosophy, existence displays a variety of ineradicable and irreducible forms within which meaningful or valid experience is expressed. Each of these forms, or basic categories, is the presupposition of the appearance of a variety of cultural and historical facts that exist as the content-determined ways in which the universality and necessity of the basic laws of life are made visible, objective and concrete. Corresponding to the variety of religious expressions that characterize history is the religious *a priori*; to the variety of ethical attitudes and dispositions, the basic ethical category; to aesthetic phenomena, the aesthetic fundamental form; and, finally to the realm of knowledge and ideas, the noetic context of meaning.

Philosophy, according to this neo-Kantian theory, regards these above-mentioned forms as the channels through which man fills his life with meaningfulness. The fundamental theory of being that lies at the heart of this epistemology regards being *qua* being, or being outside of and prior to the processes of culture and history, as raw matter or pure objectivity. Meaning is then strictly dependent upon the concrete and determinate material of history that men create through the various forms of objectification.

The religions, or religious phenomena, are concrete materials through which *ultimate* meaningfulness (the reconciliation of the infinite with the finite) is conferred upon history. The religious life of man is typified by the fact that in it the infinite manifests itself to man. Religion is, therefore, the reality or domain of *absolute* meaningfulness that raises man above space and time and places him in the sphere of *eternity*.

According to Nygren, men in human history have
formed a variety of such principles of ultimate validity.
Agape is the one identified by the Christian church.
Nygren's specific language here is that *Agape* is Christianity's *fundamental motif,* the one reality in terms of
which the Christian faith identifies itself, or differentiates itself from alternative experiences of the presence of the infinite in the finite. *Agape* is the one
constant that confers upon the historical and cultural
variables of the Christian church their individuality,
identifiability and distinctiveness. Furthermore, since
the Christian ethos flows from the Christian commitment,
Agape is said to fully describe and to regulate the Christian's relationship to his neighbor and to the larger
world. Finally, *Nomos* and *Eros* are similarly *fundamental
motifs*. Each define alternative frameworks in terms of
which others in the human community form alternative,
though equally valid, religious experience.

It is at this point that we can introduce a few of
the key dimensions of Wingren's evaluation. Nygren's
claim that *Agape, Nomos* and *Eros* constitute equally ultimate and equally valid varieties of religious experience
is supported, according to Wingren and contrary to Nygren's own assertion, by a value-laden concrete commitment
and scheme. Specifically, this is the form-matter (or
form-content) scheme of the neo-Kantian philosophy. This
scheme requires that content can only be a human, cultural
and historical product. Furthermore, it requires that
content—for example, the Christian content—can only
function within the sphere and dynamic of the *spiritual*
life. This means that any specific content is objectified
spirit or self-consciousness become fact. Operating within the domain of self-consciousness alone, the motifs and

the limited historical material that each defines are
only subjective forms of validity.

   Wingren's major contention against Nygren is therefore that the so-called "universal element" of Nygren's
philosophy (or the element of universal and necessary
normativity) eclipses the Christian content. In neo-
Kantianism, a principle of universality by definition
cannot belong to the Christian content because the Christian content is one among several. However, there is,
according to Wingren, a "universal element" in Christianity itself, namely, "creation and law." For Wingren, the
eclipse of creation within Nygren's position is noticeable at various levels.

   First, by definition the "universal element" is
placed outside of the framework of the Christian content.
It is itself a non-Christian fundamental motif. Since
the "universal element" does not belong to the Christian
content, it appears only as a limited historical datum.
In the neo-Kantian perspective, a content representing
decision and commitment cannot be allowed to be present
in a formal scientific analysis. (It must be remembered
that for Nygren and neo-Kantian philosophy, scientific
truth and faith commitment define separate contexts of
meaning.)

   Yet in the total Nygren system *there is* a specific
commitment and content that actually performs a formal
and scientific function. (This is the point of Wingren's
persistent accusation in *Theology in Conflict* that Nygren's philosophy of religion lacks radical formality.)
As is obvious to non-neo-Kantians, there is an identifi-
able historical material present in Nygren's philosophic
analyses. And this material is Nygren's own operative
systematic perspective. In Nygren's own systematic perspective there is an operative "universal element," but

it is intrinsic to his philosophical commitments and not
to his theology.

The upshot of Wingren's critique at this level is,
then, that not *every* *Nomos* has been turned into a limited
historical material by Nygren. Radical formality or universality and necessity are claimed for the expressed
philosophy of the cultural forms. Radical formality is
thus tacitly credited *only* to the unexpressed and historically relative concept of reality-as-raw-matter-for-
human-form-giving to which the neo-Kantian philosophy is
systematically tied. Unbeknownst to himself, Nygren has
created a formal philosophical disguise for a certain
limited historical material and philosophic commitment.

Second, there is also a related level at which the
so-called "universal element" is dropped from the discussion. *Nomos* and *Agape* are defined as distinct varieties
of content as given in history. Neither defines the "form"
of religion itself, for a form is allegedly not determined
by content. This means that neither *Nomos* nor *Agape* are
universally valid in the sense of truthful objectivity.
Nomos and *Agape* are decisional and dispositional frameworks within the spiritual life of the Jewish and Christian communities respectively. *Nomos* does not have normative significance for the Christian community; *Agape* has
no normative significance for the Jewish fellowship. For
scientific theology, *Nomos* and *Agape* are simply the historically distinct ways in which two communities form
valid religious experience. Each motif is a way in which
the collective self-consciousness (spirit) of the community has come to religious expression. *Nomos* and *Agape* are
two religious symbolisms and the self-assertions of two
separate communities.

From a neo-Kantian perspective, scientific theology
can neither say that *Nomos* is a supra-arbitrary criterion

of continuity (or law) to which *all* (Jews and Christians
and old men alike) are related, nor that *Agape* is a radical demand (or law) placed upon *all*. Scientific theology cannot say that the demand of love (*Agape*) is natural
and given with life itself, for this would in effect be
a confusion of form and content, of universality and historical particularity.

Exactly this signal fact—that *Nomos* and *Agape* are
required by the alleged pure formality of Nygren's philosophy to be merely content-determined forms of subjective
validity—is the basis of Wingren's major criticism of
Nygren. For, according to Wingren, there are "...defi-
nite historical realities, definite elements in the
structure of the biblical word, which become obscured when
the biblical writings are assumed to contain 'religious
propositions,'"[43] or to be supported by fundamental motifs.
According to Wingren, the Lundensian theology is wrong in
its historical approach, and Wingren has argued that intrinsic but unexamined philosophical assumptions have
brought this about. From Wingren's perspective, a revision of the entire Lundensian philosophy is required.

Limitations of space prevent a similar extensive
analysis of Wingren's rejection of prevailing philosophies
of existence. With Einar Billing, Wingren interprets the
Logical Positivism of Axel Hägerström as eclipsing "the
universal element" by being bound to a nineteenth and
twentieth century fact-value dualism. In this framework
scientific philosophy and theology must view the Christian
faith as a collection of religious propositions, a system
of belief concepts.[44] As I have said at the beginning of
this section, the dialectical Existentialism of Kierkegaard and his followers, among whom Wingren counts Barth
and Bultmann, also merits similar opposition for eclipsing
the biblical view of creation and law.

At this point a word of caution must be expressed about the proper sense of this negativism towards philosophy in the Wingren *corpus*. The conclusion must not be drawn that Wingren is anti-philosophical as such. Rather, the point is that Wingren has rejected prevailing options concerning the relationship of philosophy and theology. Indeed, only the search for more adequate non-theological analyses can explain Wingren's increasing dependence upon the ethical and cultural philosophy of Knut Løgstrup. I shall speak directly to what it is in Løgstrup that satisfies Wingren, especially on the matter of the "universal element." But because there is so much in the Wingren *corpus* that seems to contradict the cautionary note that I have here interjected,[45] I should like briefly to point out where in the Wingren corpus I detect an *in principle* positive attitude towards philosophy that makes intelligible Wingren's attachment to Løgstrup in the last 20 years.

First, arguing in "Utläggningens problematik,"[46] ("The Problem of Hermeneutics"), an important 1950 article, that the problem of hermeneutics is the problem of the relationship of philosophy and theology, Wingren says that the concern of hermeneutics is to "attain to a *formal* philosophy that builds bridges between the content of the kerygma and other statements that we can endorse."[47] A complex concept of theological and philosophical assumptions is clearly present here. Furthermore, philosophy seems to be more than just a threat to theology. Both seem in principle capable of neutrality with respect to one another. Indeed, philosophy may play a positive role in building bridges between the kerygma and culture, as Wingren later discovered in relation to Løgstrup.

Thus Wingren's view of the relationship of philosophy to theology becomes clearer. Wingren does not

regard philosophy as such as inimical to theology. Win-
grin only rejects those philosophies that fail to be
totally "neutral" or "formal" with respect to the biblical material. Philosophy may not harbor a content that
is inappropriate to the normative perspective of Scripture.

Second, in Wingren's book on Einar Billing, a most
illuminating discussion appears in the seventh chapter,
which is entitled "A Neglected Problem: The Relationship
between Theology and Philosophy." In this section Wingren refers frequently to Billing's indifference to philosophy and his similarity to Barth on this matter. Wingren writes, "He [Billing] refused to deal with the relationship between philosophy and theology, and constantly avoided this task."[48] In fact Billing is said to have
openly expressed a hesitant attitude to contemporary philosophers, particularly Axel Hägerström and the Swedish
school of Logical Positivism. According to Wingren,
Billing "spoke out clearly and intentionally...in...his
disapproval of Hägerström and Nygren."[49] Because Billing
knew only this philosophy and some German Idealism and was
sceptical of both, Billing left the problem of the relationship of philosophy and theology alone.

Billing is known in theology mostly for his work in
Old Testament studies. The peculiarity of Billing in com-
parison to classical patterns is, according to Wingren,
Billing's focus on Israel and its historical experiences.
The foundation of the Old Testament is, thus, located by
Billing in the Exodus event.

Strikingly enough, it is exactly Billing's Exodus
orientation that Wingren now associates with Billing's
silence on philosophy. Billing refuses to begin biblically and theologically with the Genesis pre-history. Yet
unexpressed in Billing's discussion of the Exodus there

appears, according to Wingren, "a universal element,"
for there is the express assertion that the church *today*
brings the same forgiveness and deliverance to its people. Comments Wingren: Had Billing become alert to this
dimension, to this assumption that creation, humanity and
its conscience are weighed down by sin, he would have
been led back directly to the Genesis starting-point. According to Wingren, Billing would have had to take up the
question of creation and law and would thereby have discovered a perspective that could perform the legitimate
function of a philosophical anthropology. Writes Wingren,
"The *presuppositions* of all his [Billing's] work involved
an anthropology in which the concepts of creation and
guilt were fundamental."[50] As is, Billing's hesitance
about Idealism and Logical Positivism and Billing's orientation to the Exodus story prevent a consideration of the
relationship of theology and philosophy. However, "If
one takes the thought of creation seriously," Wingren
concludes, "one cannot in the long run avoid dealing with
the relationship between philosophy and theology."[51]

    · From the above remarks it becomes clear that the Gos-
pel in Wingren's view requires explication in terms of definite assumptions. The question at issue would be whether,
according to Wingren, those assumptions are strictly theological, coming from Revelation, or whether they can be
philosophical as well. The discussions in "Utläggningens
problematik" and in the book on Billing seem to confirm
the latter. Hence, it is now possible to turn to Wingren's
association with Løgstrup, since it is here that Wingren
finds his philosophy.

    The connection with Løgstrup evidences the further
conviction not only that these assumptions *can* possibly be
philosophical, but also that they *must* necessarily be so.
An analysis positively directed to natural structures is

needed. Against the Barthian alternative to Nygren's
system, Wingren is confident that a repetition of the
Christian *gnosis* or a speculative development of biblical
concepts (such as Christ) as philosophic categories is
inadequate. Or in Wingren's own words, "A theological
concept such as 'natural law' really cries out for a
purely philosophical analysis."[52]

The only requirement or control that must be imposed on this philosophical analysis is that it be "neutral" or "open" to the Christian content in its entirety.
This is not openness or neutrality in general, but an
openness determined by the very content under consideration. Only in this way can the "universal element" be
both described historically and utilized systematically.

The consequence for theology is that it will not
be hindered in viewing the "universal element" as the presupposition of *Agape*. Furthermore, it will be possible
to regard *Nomos* as an actual condition of normativity in
which all men stand irrespective of their grasp of reality. And, finally, *Agape* too will be able to be recognized as a demand, a *Nomos* or natural law that is placed
upon all. A philosophy that allows this does not deprive
the Christian faith of part of its belief content, but can
rather be said to be "neutral" with respect to it. Where
Nygren's neo-Kantianism, Hägerström's Logical Positivism,
and Bultmann's Existentialism have been found wanting by
Wingren exactly on this score, Løgstrup's philosophy of
the Sovereign Life Expressions is, according to Wingren,
adequate. Wingren himself describes what has led to his
own positive appraisal of Løgstrup's thought:

> The task [to provide a purely philosophical analysis
> of a theological content such as 'natural law'] is
> there waiting but I pass it by. My excuse is that,
> despite many years of searching, I have found no
> philosopher, neither analytical nor existential,

whom I could take over directly. I am not capable
myself of constructing a philosophy from the very
foundations. I can only hope that the topics I
leave aside will be dealt with by other writers.
What Løgstrup at Aarhus has written in recent
years seems to me, even by international standards,
to be among the most interesting works in this
field.[53]

It is not surprising, then, that there has been in
the Wingren *corpus* a growing affirmation of Løgstrup's
philosophy, at least since 1958 (*Creation and Law*).[54]
For Wingren, the Christian *gnosis*, or the Christian belief content has proven not to have been enough. Wingren's
contribution to an adequate understanding of that content
itself has been to affirm that it points beyond itself to
"the universal element." That is, a part of the belief
content is directly related to what transcends every belief system. In his own almost exclusive dependence upon
theological language, interrupted only by occasional attempts to "do some 'sifting'...or 'screening' among the
'multitudes of demands,'"[55] Wingren detects a tendency of
theological language to generate a life of its own that
leads us away from reality. Løgstrup has helped Wingren
see that the Christian content, even if and when expanded
to include creation and law, cannot be an alternative to
a positive analysis of anthropological and ontic structures.
Even though the biblical idea of creation and law must function as a controlling belief for any analysis, philosophy
is needed to provide a concrete analysis of the domain of
the demands and to talk a universal language that speaks to
all men.

Partially in response to the intrinsic difficulties
of Lundensian motif research and partially in relation to
Wingren's longstanding dissatisfaction with purely Christocentric theology and ethics, a new theological orientation
has emerged in Lund. This new orientation is furthermore

closely tied to the new theological and philosophical al-
liance that has developed between Wingren in Lund and
Løgstrup in Aarhus. So intimate has the contact become
that much intense scientific study of Løgstrup's works
has been executed in Lund.[56] In addition Wingren himself
was awarded a honorary doctorate at Aarhus in the fall of
1978.

We must in the final section consider especially the
orientation to creation that underlies the dissatisfaction
of Wingren and Løgstrup with prevailing cultural idealisms,
analytical positivisms, and existentialist philosophies.
We must try to explain the concern of both to assert human
solidarity in every area of life on the basis of creation.
This orientation towards creation is directed primarily
against subjectivism's identification of life with the
various human consciousnesses of it and against the theological gnosticism of Christocentrism and *Offenbarungs-*
positivismus.

In this connection, Løgstrup's development of the
doctrine of creation through the idea of the so-called
"Sovereign Life Expressions" is basic.[57] Nearly every reference to Løgstrup in Wingren's works centers on this philosophic concept of Løgstrup and its attendant implications.[58]
For Wingren, attachment to this Løgstrupian idea has meant
that "creation" has come to stand for the given context
structure of Life. Consequently, Wingren has also come to
refer frequently to the fact of the givenness of life as
"the universal element." According to this approach, all
persons everywhere, irrespective of the faith and grasp of
reality they have in mind, receive the gift of Life. Even
outside of the acceptance of this or that faith, human life
is a dialogue in which the "universal element" is present.
Furthermore, this term, common to all, is God's act of creation and the determinate order of existence that God's act

sustains. Within this structured context, which is the
form of God's continuing presence in the creation, all
persons make their religious choices and form their ethical practices.

On this basis Wingren and Løgstrup refuse to acknowledge that it is right and scientific to regard the
religions and various ethical self-assertions of men as
operating within the dynamic of history, culture, and
subjectivity alone. Creation is not "raw matter" or
"pure possibility" for autonomous, meaning-conferring
beings. According to Løgstrup and Wingren, such a view
of creation is reflective of a private, content-determined
Cultural Idealistic view of life and man. By contrast,
for Wingren and Løgstrup, creation is the universal experience of divine presence as the inescapable experience of
the goodness and order of Life.

A major implication of this conception of Life as
Sovereign having certain universal and trans-subjective
manifestations in the lives of all, is that the realm sepa-
rating the religions and self-assertions of men from one
another is a common or shared experience; it is not a vacuum. Moreover, every life expression (fear, or trust, or
guilt, or confidence, or despair, or hope) is a dialogue
with this common link. Hence, Wingren and Løgstrup imply
that as we reflect upon the various self-assertions of
man, we must regard them not just as assertions of the
self, but as expressions of the one Life we all share.
There is, according to Wingren and Løgstrup, a certain
basic "common sense" to every expression of faith and life
and this "common sense" is the basis of analogy among the
various experiences of men. Without such a "common sense"
there can be no analogy and without an analogy of life
there can be no meaningful understanding, no meaningful,
faithful, trustful, human, and decent civil human praxis.

4. Conclusion

I shall conclude this essay with a few questions for Wingren and Løgstrup. On the basis of those
questions I will offer a suggestion as to where I think
Wingren will be pressed to move from here. Wingren has
criticized Nygren for tying theology to a philosophical
structure that is not neutral with respect to the Christian content. Løgstrup's positive analysis seems to
Wingren to fulfill his requirement of philosophical neutrality, whereas the purely Christomonistic fideism of
Barth (and Kierkegaard) seems increasingly untenable.
Yet it seems that Wingren does not acknowledge often
enough that the "openness" of Løgstrup's philosophy to
the whole Christian content is itself a lack of radical
formality. Even Wingren seems to fall back on the long-
standing Lutheran propensity to interpret the radical
demand and the "universal element" as unaided reason, or
consensus, that operates in the philosophical and civil
spheres. One might query whether there is in Wingren a
proper sensitivity to the *Christian Lutheran* concrete-
ness of Løgstrup's conceptuality.

As all can readily see, Løgstrup speaks positively
about the anthropological structure (the "universal element") without attempting to extract it from Christology
or even from the whole of the Christian or biblical belief content. Løgstrup is a philosopher and draws on
and analyzes the data with which all must deal in the
search for what being means. Yet clearly Løgstrup thinks,
weighs and devises theories by means of *his own* reason,
a reason unmistakeably embedded in a *Lutheran Christian*
inheritance.

The question that I wish to ask here is whether the
idea of the "universal element" and the "Sovereign Life
Expressions" is not in danger of coming to support again

the idea of rational objectivity in philosophy and human
consensus in society. This latter concept of philosophy
and practical reason has been tried in the modern centuries and the modern critiques of reason have amply demonstrated what deficiencies are involved here. Is not a
deficiency of the Løgstrup (Wingren?) approach the fact
that the idea of creation, which is the idea of a shared
Life-World, runs the risk of leading to the assumption of
a shared and common *grasp* of that shared and common world?
Stated in terms of the modern theological debate as sharply focused by Barth, a serious question here is whether
Wingren's recovery of creation from its renunciation by
the convulsive attack of neo-Orthodoxy on modernism and
secularism can avoid falling prey to the virus of natural
theology and natural knowledge.

It does seem unclear to Løgstrup (and maybe even to
Wingren too)[59] whether it is possible to affirm and begin
the philosophic task with the "universal element" and
"the Sovereign Life Expressions" and yet at one and the
same time to affirm that the "universal element" is con-
cretely what the Christian biblical revelation describes
as "creation and law." Where the attempt directly to
extract reality from the Christian belief content is rejected by Wingren and Løgstrup, both seem to think that
every "Christian Ethic" or "Christian Philosophy" must
be denounced as well.[60]

Aiming at extrication from a subjectivistic view of
religious faith and ethical praxis (Nygren) and from a
view of Revelation as Christian *gnosis* unwarranted and
unindicated in any way whatsoever by "natural Life"
(Barth and Kierkegaard), Wingren and Løgstrup have yet to
properly relate creation to the reality of Revelation.
Our real concern should be whether they can, since, oddly
enough, as for Nygren so too for Wingren and Løgstrup, it

seems that "Revelation" remains viewed as a distinctly Christian *form of consciousness*. (For example, the concept of "Revelation" gets negatively associated by Løgstrup and Wingren with the Barthian view and use of it as a kind of second order "special ideology" or "Christian *gnosis*.")[61]

To Wingren and Løgstrup we must then address this question: does it not seem possible both to affirm creation and yet to give an account of Revelation without swallowing that Revelation up into a naturally and universally available common sense? This central question as to how creation as human solidarity can be affirmed without a sacrifice of the distinctiveness of Christian Revelation remains unsettled in Lundensian thought as a whole. Surely it remains unsettled in Løgstrup's thought. Maybe the future contact of Wingren with non-Scandinavian theologians who have developed their commitment to the uniqueness of Christian Revelation beyond Barthian and Germanic theology will bring about some new settlement of the knotty problem of creation and its relation to the reality of Christian Revelation. Viewed in relation to these unsettled questions, Wingren's tour in North America in January and February of 1979 surely promises to be an exciting theological dialogue. In fact, the overall title of Wingren's lectures—Creation and Gospel—shows that it is exactly this problem (with the modification that for Wingren the term "Gospel" is used in the place of "Revelation") that Wingren has come to see as *the* issue for the further development of his own and Løgstrup's valuable creation-oriented thought.

FOOTNOTES

[1] Wingren, *Flight from Creation* (Minneapolis, 1971), p. 15.

[2] Wingren, "Irenaeus och Marcion. Studier över Skapelsetanken," unpublished licentiate thesis (Lund, 1939).

[3] Wingren, "Was geschah eigentlich in Lund in den dreissiger Jahren?" *Theologische Literaturzeitung*, 97 (1972), p. 889.

[4] The dissertation was published in Swedish in 1942 and in English in 1947, under the title *Luther on Vocation* in the U.S. and under the title *The Christian's Calling* in Britain.

[5] Wingren, "Was geschah," pp. 885-86.

[6] Aulén, G., *Christus Victor: An Historical Study of the Three Main Types of the Idea of the Atonement* (New York, 1960).

[7] Nygren, A., *Agape and Eros* (Philadelphia, 1953). Nygren's 2 volume work is the major classic example of Lundensian Theology and the method of historical motif research.

[8] Bring, R., *Till frågan om den systematiska teologiens uppgift* (Lund, 1933). No English translation of this work exists.

[9] Wingren himself briefly describes the formation of the Lundensian "School" in the thirties in the following manner: "The legacy from Uppsala that Aulén had contributed became weaker. Furthermore, the importance of Bring's fundamental work in methodology increased, and systematic theology accordingly became historical analysis. In addition, philosophy was no longer pursued because it had already, through the work of Nygren and Bring, had its effect on theology by forcing it to be turned into history. It is at this point that the Lundensians begin to work historically with the source materials (Luther, Thomas, Irenaeus, etc.) Thus, the standards for systematic theology became the historical sources themselves." ("Was geschah," p. 888). Translation: Henry Vander Goot.

[10]"Marcions kristendomstolkning," *Svensk Teologisk Kvartalskrift,* 12 (1936), 318-38. (Hereafter, *STK*).

[11]"Skapelsen, lagen och inkarnationen enligt Irenaeus," *STK*, 16 (1940), 133-55. See also his "Frälsningens Gud såsom skapare och domare," *STK,* 16 (1940), 322-39.

[12]"Den springande punkten," *STK*, 3 (1974), p. 101. Translation: Henry Vander Goot.

[13]*Flight from Creation,* p. 15.

[14]Wingren, *The Living Word* (Philadelphia, 1960), p. 84.

[15]*Theology in Conflict* (Philadelphia, 1958), p. 161, and *Creation and Law* (Philadelphia, 1961), p. 189.

[16]"Den springande punkten," p. 102. Translation: Henry Vander Goot.

[17]*The Living Word,* p. 83.

[18]Hall, Thor, *Framework for Faith: Lundensian Theological Methodology in the Thought of Ragnar Bring* (Leiden, 1970), p. 229.

[19]"Utläggningens problematik," *STK*, 26 (1950), p. 404, N.1. Translation: Henry Vander Goot.

[20]"Was geschah," p. 889. Translation: Henry Vander Goot.

[21]"Filosofi och teologi hos biskop Nygren," *STK*, 32 (1956), pp. 295-6. Translation: Henry Vander Goot.

[22]*Ibid.,* p. 296. Translation: Henry Vander Goot.

[23]*Flight from Creation,* p. 19.

[24]*Ibid.,* pp. 19-20.

[25]Cf. "Filosofi och teologi hos biskop Nygren," p. 304, where Wingren comments on learning from Continental theology that historical science does not exhaust the theologian's work. The task of systematic theology lies beyond. To ignore this is to ignore the changing historical circumstances in which we live, circumstances in terms of which and with reference to which the Word must always be

stated anew. Cf. n. 25 and n. 20 above.

[26]*Flight from Creation,* p. 20.

[27]Thus we can say that next to Wingren's opposition
to the Lundensian theology and certain developments in the
Swedish Church, Wingren's *Auseinandersetzung* with Karl
Barth is one of the most crucial, historical dimensions
involved in understanding the fundamentality of creation
(the first article of the Apostles' Creed) in the theology
of Gustaf Wingren.

[28]"Den springande punkten," p. 102. Translation:
Henry Vander Goot.

[29]*Ibid.,* pp. 101 and 104.

[30]*Ibid.,* p. 102. Translation: Henry Vander Goot.

[31]"Några karakteristiska drag i modern teologi,"
STK, 27 (1951), pp. 144-5.

[32]Nygren, A., "Til teologiens metodfråga, *STK,* 32
(1956), pp. 20-35.

[33]Wingren, G., "Teologiens metodfråga," *STK,* 32
(1956), pp. 36-41.

[34]Wingren, G., *STK,* 32 (1956), pp. 122-32.

[35]Nygren, A., *STK,* 32 (1956), pp. 133-60.

[36]Wingren, G., *STK,* 32 (1956), pp. 284-312.

[37]Nygren, A., "Slutreplik angaende teologiens
metodfråga," *STK,* 32 (1956), pp. 313-22.

[38]Cf. A. Nygren, *Meaning and Method: Prolegomena to
a Scientific Philosophy and a Scientific Theology* (Philadelphia, 1972).

[39]Wingren, *An Exodus theology, Einar Billing and
the Development of Modern Swedish Theology* (Philadelphia,
1969), pp. 153-4.

[40]Cf. the chapters in *Theology in Conflict* on Barth
and Bultmann. Cf. also the critical and negative evaluation of both Cullmann and Bultmann in *Creation and Law,* pp.
68-72. The negative assessment of Kierkegaard's influence
is scattered throughout Wingren's work and is heavily de-

pendent upon Løgstrup's *Opgør med Kierkegaard*. Wingren's chief concern is Kierkegaard's "gnostic" opposition of Christ to the so-called "natural manifestations of life." This nihilistic tendency is, according to Wingren, picked up especially by Barth c.s. Cf. *Flight from Creation*, p. 20, where Barth is described as the "spiritual father" of the "modern negation of belief in creation."

[41]Hall laments the prospects for the future of reflection on methodological questions in theology. He regards the "dirth of new leadership in Lundensian methodology...as a consequence of the great impact of dialectic theology" which considers "methodology...as part of an exclusively doctrinal orientation" (*Framework*, p. 206). Furthermore, because "dialectic commitments dominate Wingren's attempt to recapture theological methodology within an unquestioning reliance upon biblical categories of thought represents an unfortunate return to the philosophical naiveté of the precritical age," (p. 215) Hall predicts that "he will not inspire younger scholars to take up the methodological task left by his predecessor and his former colleague in Lund" (p. 211). (The references are to Nygren and Bring respectively.)

[42]"Filosofi och teologi hos biskop Nygren," p. 296.

[43]*Theology in Conflict*, p. 92.

[44]"Värderingar inom den systematiska teologin," *STK*, 48 (1972), pp. 30-31; and "Den springande punkten," *STK*, p. 105.

[45]The constructive claim of *Theology in Conflict*, namely that "if the task is to work with a certain content, the method has to be defined as we work with that content, not before that contact has been made," seems to lend credence to the frequent association of Wingren's position on method in theology with the view of Karl Barth, who resists every attempt to permit an alien discipline like philosophy to decree the nature and structure of the gospel. Also, in *Creation and Law* we do indeed witness occasional attempts to place the New Testament over against philosophical anthropologies. For example, this attitude is glimpsed in the following expressions: (a) "Barth, Bultmann and Nygren give little place in their theology to the Old Testament, and work rather with philosophical presuppositions"; and (b) "In isolation from the Old Testament it is in danger of evolving a philosophical anthropology," (pp. 15 and 17 respectively). In this context Wingren does not consider whether the Old Testament is itself a right

philosophical anthropology. Nor does Wingren ask whether
and how the Old Testament could give rise to such a right
philosophical anthropology, and, hence, how it is meaningful to place the Old Testament *over against* philosophy as
such. Furthermore, the position of *Theology in Conflict*
("that the question of method must be settled solely by
reference to the subject-matter with which theology has to
deal") is repeated to make clear to the reader that Wingren's primary concern is the *content* of theology.

[46]"Utläggningens problematik," *STK*, 26 (1950), pp.
403-12.

[47]*Ibid.*, p. 411.

[48]Wingren, G., *An Exodus Theology*, p. 148.

[49]*Ibid.*, 149.

[50]*Ibid.*, p. 153.

[51]*Ibid.*, p. 160.

[52]Wingren, G., *Flight from Creation*, p. 29.

[53]*Loc. cit.*

[54]In *Creation and Law* Wingren's stress on the universality and objectivity of the Law is supported by frequent references to Løgstrup's work. Cf. for example,
pp. 29-31. In the succeeding years an even more positive
affirmation of Løgstrup's work becomes evident. Cf.
especially Wingren's "Mina ämnesval. Apologia pro vita mea.
Teologisk självporträtt," *Var lösen*, 57 (1966), pp. 494-
500. This autobiographical sketch appeared in English
translation in 1971 as Chapter 1 of Wingren's *Flight from
Creation*. For understanding Wingren's attraction to
Løgstrup as related to the rejection of the Christocentric ethics of the Barthians, cf. especially his 1970
article in *Neue Zeitschrift für Systematische Theologie
und Religionsphilosophie*, 12, pp. 184-95. This article
appears in English translation as the second chapter of
Flight from Creation and is there entitled "Creation and
Theology. Theology between Dogmatics and Analysis." Especially on pp. 60-66 neo-Orthodox attempts to extract ethics
from Christology and to place the revelation in Christ over
against a positive anthropology as based on creation are
characterized as "nihilistic" and, following Løgstrup,
associated with the influence of Kierkegaard's dialectical
Existentialism.

[55]Wingren, *Flight from Creation,* p. 62.

[56]Cf. e.g., the fact that one of Wingren's most competent doctoral students (Lars-Olle Armgard) has completed in recent years (1971) a very significant dissertation for the University of Lund on Løgstrup's thought: *Antropologi: Problem I K.E. Løgstrup's Forfattarskap* (Lund, 1971).

[57]This idea is especially extensively developed in Løgstrup's *The Ethical Demand* (Philadelphia, 1971). Cf. e.g., pp. 111f. This work is, moreover, the one work by Løgstrup that has influenced Wingren most. One of the next most significant works is Løgstrup's *Opgør med Kierkegaard* (Kobenhavn, 1968), which appears in German translation under the title *Auseinandersetzung mit Kierkegaard* (München, 1968).

[58]Cf. *Creation and Law,* pp. 47, 50, 63, 157; *Gospel and Church* (Philadelphia, 1964), pp. 118-19, 175, 184, 228; *Flight from Creation,* pp. 29, 42-5, 63, 70; *Credo. Den kristna tros-och livsåskådnungen* (Lund, 1974), pp. 25-27, 39, 43.

[59]By distinguishing Løgstrup from Wingren here, I intend to indicate that though Wingren and Løgstrup have grown closer in recent years, in times past Wingren has himself raised critical questions about Løgstrup's view of the Sovereign Life Expressions or Orders—questions that resemble my own as directed to both thinker's alike. For example, in *Creation and Law* Wingren queries whether Løgstrup is strong enough in his understanding of "the critical function of the Gospel in relation to the prevailing order" (p. 165). According to Wingren—who argues this point *against* Løgstrup—"there is no radical demand which is separate from the preaching of Christ's death." (p. 189).

    In *Gospel and Church,* again Wingren argues the same point against Løgstrup. However, in this instance Wingren acknowledges that Løgstrup's denial of the relevance of a specifically "Christian" vantage point in ethics is concretely really only a denial of "that type of 'Christian ethic' which looks to scripture for its precedent in preference to becoming really involved in the problems of society where the well-being of one's neighbor is always paramount." (p. 119). Løgstrup's position is then interpreted sympathetically in terms of the specific aberration at which Løgstrup has aimed his artillery. In any case, this legitimate concern of Wingren about Løgstrup's position is not much repeated again against Løgstrup after *Gospel and Church.* After 1960 there are only a few excep-

ions: One of a minor nature appears in a 1970 article in
*Neue Zeitshrift für Systematische Theologie und Religions-
philosophie*, 12, pp. 184-95 (English: *Flight from Creation*,
p. 72); the second is a recent expression of worry and a
strong warning that creation-orientation is leading Løgstrup's students to a denial of the *uniqueness* of the Gospel ["Skapelse och evangelium," *STK*, 53 (1977), pp. 7-8].

[60]Cf. e.g., Løgstrup, *The Ethical Demand*, pp. 111-121.

[61]Cf. e.g., Wingren, *Credo*, pp. 27-32.

CREATION AND GOSPEL

THE NEW SITUATION IN EUROPEAN THEOLOGY

GUSTAF WINGREN

I. THEOLOGICAL ORIENTATION

European systematic theologians are generally exempt
from working at purely historical tasks. Often universities have one professorship in general church history and
another in the church history of their country. The theology of the Church Fathers is treated by church historians, not by systematic theologians. The same holds for
the theologies of Luther, Calvin, and others.

Sweden is an exception to this rule. The research
of its church historians is, on the one hand, almost exclusively concerned with Swedish subjects. On the other
hand, all Swedish research on Luther has been performed
by systematicians, Einar Billing being most important.
Those few books (in Sweden) that have been published on
patristic subjects have also as a rule been written by
systematic theologians, not by historians. This was originally due to the examination system, for professors of
systematics conducted examinations in the history of doctrine and the history of ideas. As far as I know, this
is the case only in Sweden and in Finland. In the rest
of Europe the subject of ecclesiastical history includes
also the history of doctrines and of ideas.

This purely external arrangement has had consider-
able effect upon Swedish systematic theology. Einar
Billing wrote a doctoral dissertation which analyzed
Luther's doctrine of the State.[1] Anders Nygren and Gustaf

Aulén created an original theology in Lund, the basis of
which was entirely historical. Aulén wrote about the
doctrine of the atonement and the image of God through
the ages; Nygren wrote about the Christian idea of Love
up to the Reformation in the sixteenth century. What was
to be the systematic substance of contemporary theology
was presented by certain epochs which were described as
"successful" in their attempt to determine what is
"Christian," while other epochs were described as less
successful. Aulén and Nygren were agreed on their choice
of the "successful" epochs: those represented most bril-
liantly by Irenaeus and Luther.

   Nygren knew of no interpreters of the idea of Love
who surpassed Irenaeus and Luther. In the same way,
Aulén considered Irenaeus and Luther to be uniquely clear
representatives of that doctrine of atonement which he
called "classical." The research results of Nygren and
Aulén were presented in Lund in the 1930s, specifically
in the years 1930 and 1936.[2]

   I began my theological studies in 1930, passed my
first examination in 1935, and started my studies for the
doctorate in theology in 1936. It goes without saying
that the books that were published by my teachers at the
university exercised a strong influence on me. The works
of Aulén and Nygren were later translated into several
languages and have been received worldwide as the most
important contributions of Swedish theology to international theological debate.

   One must realize how strongly these two Swedish
theologians concentrated on Christology, the Second Article of the Apostles' Creed. In this respect Aulén and
Nygren parallel Karl Barth. In another respect, however,
they were diametrically opposed to Barth, for they did
not accept the kerygmatic approach, which he shared with

Rudolf Bultmann. Aulén and Nygren were essentially historians, perhaps because of the above mentioned examination system in Sweden. Other factors also played a role.

In no country, at least not in any of those in the
northern part of Europe, have the attacks on theology
been as violent as in Sweden. In the first place, the
criticism has been that theology is not strictly scientific. But since no one can reasonably deny that a historical description of a long-existing faith is scientific work, the Swedish theologians were driven, in sheer
self-defense, to adopt a strictly historical approach
which departed from the kerygmatically-oriented tasks of
systematic theologians in other countries. Practical theology, incidentally, developed in the same direction in
Sweden: it too confined itself to historical tasks.

What is of special interest in this connection is
Aulén's and Nygren's positive evaluation of Irenaeus and
Luther, the one an anti-Gnostic Father of the Early Church
and the other an aggressively anti-monastic reformer of
the sixteenth century. Irenaeus was ardently Christological in his anthropology and thereby also in his conception
of salvation (soteriology). Luther had the same focus:
Christology and the doctrine of justification were central
in his theology.

Aulén and Nygren also centered on these subjects.
It was with these problems before them that they read
Irenaeus and Luther, and it was with these spectacles on
that they made their selection of historical texts. Indeed, their work was selective, being directed by the
same problems that on the Continent moved Barth to develop
an entirely different type of theology.

One could, on reading Irenaeus and Luther, take an
interest in other subjects. Irenaeus' chief enemy was
Gnosticism and, in particular, Marcion. Irenaeus asserted

against the Gnostics that God created the earth and gave
the Law. He therefore also described salvation as the
"restoration" of man (*recapitulatio*)—a completion of
God's decision to create. Luther strove vigorously
against the monastic ideal, for he wished to give the
worldly vocations a position of honor as the only "spiritual" callings in the life of the Christian: for Luther
the world was the place where it is possible to serve
one's neighbor and live in the imitation of Christ. Note
that all of these thoughts were developed by Irenaeus and
Luther in the course of an interpretation of the First
Article of the Creed (concerning Creation) and were carried out with astonishing boldness.

If a young theologian would search through the historical sources from the beginning of church history to
the present for these authors who have with the greatest
intensity and force set forth the meaning of faith in
Creation, authors who have been able to integrate that
faith with the message of salvation in Christ, he would
have to choose Irenaeus and Luther, for they stressed the
doctrine of Creation as do no other theologians. Moreover,
in Irenaeus and Luther the doctrine of Creation was built
into the doctrines of Christ, the Gospel, the sacraments,
and eschatology with unparalleled consistency.

Yet Aulén and Nygren describe the doctrine of atonement and the idea of Love in Irenaeus and in Luther without giving to the First Article of the Creed the place
that is its due. This is undoubtedly evidence of a dependence on contemporary continental theology, since the
theological atmosphere in Europe in the 1930s was dominated
by Christology and ecclesiology.[3]

What is often overlooked, however, is the relationship between this modern atmosphere on the one hand and
Pietism, the Revivalist Movements, Søren Kierkegaard, and

older phenomena on the other. After the demise of Liberal theology at the end of World War I, European university theologians generally reestablished the connection
with older ways of thinking that were alien to Liberalism
but nonetheless akin to Pietistic ideas. (In Pietism
there is the idea of something human, something that is
not yet "Christian;" then alongside this basic humanity
there appears a specifically Christian faith and a special form of life built on the Gospel. Hence, systematic
theologians analyze the specifically Christian as distinct from what is generally human.) As a reaction
against Liberal theology this development around 1920 is
understandable, for liberalism had identified Christianity with a prevailing European *Bildungsreligion*—cultural
religion—to the detriment of the Gospel and Christology.
But compared to the Reformation and the time of the Church
Fathers, all modern theology (Barth, Bultmann, Aulén,
Nygren) represents a serious loss of substance.

This loss of substance may be most simply expressed
in the following way. During the classical epochs of
Christian history it was impossible to speak of anything
as good without viewing it as received from the hand of
God. Food, sunshine, care of the sick, health friendship:
all of this was seen as coming—if it was good—from God,
and could not be thought to have come from anyone else.
All things could indeed be distorted and become destructive, but in that case nothing could be construed as
"generally human." On the contrary, it would have to be
seen as diabolical and as defying God.

This view of life cannot be articulated on the basis of the Second Article of the Creed alone. It is necessary to have recourse to the First Article of Faith (Creation) in order to articulate this view of life. The
doctrine of Creation may very well be included in the

Second and Third Articles of Faith——in the doctrines of
Christ and of the Holy Ghost. But it is not possible to
construct a comprehensive view of the biblical faith only
on the basis of the two later Articles of Faith to the
neglect of the First.

It is a mistake to think that the preservation of
the comprehensive view is simply an academic issue. Quite
the contrary, it is of great concern for the people. Indeed, it is of vital significance for the church to present this comprehensive view carefully and reasonably
when the church approaches ordinary people with the Gospel. The less priestly the milieu, the more everyday
life is dominated by work and the elementary needs of
life. Accordingly, for these people, the factors I mention must become the normal concerns of the life of faith
——must become those parts of existence with which faith
in God wrestles, namely food, illness, health, friendship,
deceit, love, and death. Faith can in no way live as
faith unless these elementary factors of existence are
viewed in the context of faith or endured in faith. The
church is paralyzed in its practical work of preaching
the Gospel if it lacks the First Article of Faith and
preaches only the Second and the Third.

I came from an environment that was not in the least
priestly. In my whole family there was no one who had any
more education in theological subjects than what the elementary school offered. All worked with their hands in
lowly trades. I came, then, with this background to the
University of Lund, and I came there at a time when Aulén
and Nygren were both professors of systematic theology.
Furthermore, I came precisely at the time when their most
important work, later internationally circulated and discussed, saw the light of day.

My interest in the First Article of Faith and the

idea of Creation would under all circumstances have taken
me to Irenaeus and to Luther. At the same time, precisely Irenaeus and Luther were identified by my teachers as
preeminent among all the interpreters of the Christian
faith in all times. Undeniably, this was a unique situation—one with a positive promise, yet one loaded with
conflict: "positive" because without much searching I immediately found the relevant historical material to study;
"loaded with conflict" because of necessity I had to apply a perspective on the material different from that applied by Aulén and Nygren. In time, open opposition developed between us.

     The delay of the conflict was related to the one-
sided historical focus of Swedish systematic theology. I
used a purely descriptive treatment of historical material
without drawing any conclusions concerning the attitude of
theology to current systematic problems, that is, without
building a dogmatic system: that was to follow later. But,
though latent, the conflict was there in the very way in
which I approached Irenaeus and Luther with Creation faith
as the main focus.

     When several people at a university are carrying on
historical studies, there may be a strange harmony and
concord among them. Even when they contextually utter
different ideas and there is multiplicity and diversity
in the scientific statements themselves, peace can be preserved. For what they are all speaking about belongs to
the past. All are one in their basic attitude: the historicizing, cool, disengaged approach. Conflict does
not arise until some person in the circle calls this attitude into question and begins to speak about method. I
will discuss this later when I give an account of my book
on preaching (1949) and my book on the question of method
(1954).[4] Actually, it was remarkable that the conflict

came as late as it did. I was appointed professor at the
University of Lund in 1951 in spite of my book on preaching, which had been published two years earlier.

The leading theologians in Sweden probably thought
that my tendencies towards criticism of the one-sided
Christological and one-sided historicizing attitude of
Swedish theology were of a temporary nature——I would soon
conform to rule again with increasing age. The only
thing that gave one a good reputation at the university
was, after all, the recognized way of working in the traditional Swedish style, a way which had been modeled with
elegance by Anders Nygren. However, as a matter of fact,
I was not especially interested in acquiring a good reputation at the university. I was, of course, pleased with
success and praise——everyone is. But in every situation
which forced me to choose between academic honor and a
vigorously functioning church, a church close to the
problems of ordinary people, I decided for the church.

The conflict with Lundensian theology was therefore
unavoidable. It was a conflict which was rooted in my
own existence, rooted in the factors that caused me as a
fifteen-year-old in a small industrial community to hit
upon the strange idea of devoting my life to theology.
The situation was aggravated, however, by a development
in the Swedish Church: a militant High Church movement
emerged during the years when I pursued my doctoral studies and wrote my first short essays. As it grew stronger,
it became focused on the clergy, thus causing the church
to be alienated from the people. An explosion had to occur——and it did——over the issue of female clergy, a question which was of interest in Sweden from the beginning
of the 1940s until its resolution in 1958. Of course the
argumentation of Anders Nygren was different from that of
High Church movement, but as far as a final stand on the

issue was concerned Nygren stood with Bo Giertz, Gustaf
Adolf Danell, and Bertil Gärtner against the ordination
of women, each of whom dissented from the eventual resolution.

It is, in my mind, a tragedy that the theology of
Anders Nygren should have led to this on the practical
plane. For, in a way, Nygren's Agape concept of the divine, sacrificing love was an extremely radical thought,
even, in principle, politically radical. And when one
thinks about that which is opposed to Agape, the radicalism becomes especially noticeable. For Agape must per-
manently resist Nomos and the legal system as a religious-
ly regulating factor on the one hand, and Eros, or love
of the self, on the other. With little exaggeration we
may say that the idea of Agape was the most radical idea
that anyone has articulated in the whole of Swedish theology in the twentieth century. But this approach has
resulted in a clearly reactionary position which is ap-
plauded by conservative groups and received with gratitude by decidedly narrow clerical circles—against a
practically unanimous worshipping congregation consisting
of the common people. This is indeed a tragedy.

It was a newsworthy event when Anders Nygren, Bishop
of the Diocese of Lund, acted as he did at the Church Synod in Stockholm in 1958. For me, however, a former doctoral
candidate in systematic theology at the University of
Lund and a former student of Nygren's who had been present when the idea of Agape was first presented in public
lectures, the tragedy of the Synod in Stockholm was not
at all surprising. This end result had had its root in
Nygren's philosophical approach, which had been established in the early 1920s.

According to this philosophy, there are necessary
questions in the history of humanity which every genera-

tion must ask. To these belong the religious question
and the ethical question. And a science that works with
exactitude can, concerning these questions, only say
that they are necessary. It is in the historically
given religions, which are full of evaluations that cannot be supported by scientific arguments, that the answers to these questions are given. Science can, however,
describe these answers in order to trace them back to
different "basic motifs." Theologians do this, for example, with respect to Christianity. In so doing they find
the basic motif Agape, which can be observed through
purely historical research. If a motif exists within the domain of the Christian faith, it cannot exist outside of Christianity.[5] Through this analysis Agape is
transformed into a distinguishing characteristic by which
the Christian faith diverges from what is human in general.

Nygren developed this argument in a learned and
philosophical manner. But its fruit did not become fully
ripe and fall from the tree until 1958, that is to say, a
whole generation later. Some fruits ripen slowly. But a
student of theology in Lund in the 1930s could even then
note that the idea of Agape in Nygren's form is a negation
of the idea of Creation. If one builds up one's philosophy as Nygren did in 1923, one treats human life as if it
were a vacuum in which no one is at work, until "the religions" come along. Faith in Creation is denied in this
philosophy. It is unavoidable that the deep radicalism
of Agape, the socially radical possibility which this
idea harbors, must be pinioned, indeed castrated, by Nygren's nihilistic philosophical framework. Even as a
young man I read this theology with boiling rage which I
in no way concealed from my theological teachers. I spoke
openly of my anger to Aulén, to Nygren, and to Ragnar Bring.

The positive dimension of these circumstances, however, lay precisely at the point where theology in Lund
was weakest, namely, in its cool, purely descriptive,
historical approach. I was able, through precisely docu-
mented historical studies, to make my way back to periods
when faith in the Creator was still alive—to the second
and sixteenth centuries, that is, to the times of Irenaeus
and to Luther. The aloof historicizing attitude of the
theological faculty had been strengthened by Aulén's move
to the Bishop's Palace at Strangnas in 1933 and his replacement by Ragnar Bring to the Chair of Dogmatics in
1934. Hence, I became a historian of ideas and wrote two
books, one on Luther (*Luther on Vocation*. Swedish, 1942),
and another on Irenaeus (*Man and the Incarnation*. Swedish,
1947).[6]

Before going into the role these two books played
in the corpus of my work, I should like to call attention
to an interesting difference between the two epochs that
I dealt with, the deep significance of which was not always as clear to me in the midst of my writing as it became later, especially toward the end of the 1960s. In
the second century the Christian church was a minority at
the center of a heathen world: those in power in Rome were
not members of the Christian community. Irenaeus did not
speak *to* them but *of* them. According to Irenaeus, the administrators of an earthly empire are tools in God's service even though they do not believe in him. In perse-
cuting the followers of Christ, however (it should be remembered that Irenaeus tasted their violence and probably
died a martyr), they demonstrated the kind of destructive
degeneration to which all administrators of earthly goods
are inclined, for example, as are parents in relation to
children and managers or foremen in relation to their
subordinates and staff. But note that what becomes harm-

ful by degeneration and distortion is in itself a good
thing.

In the sixteenth century, in contrast, the princes
were Christian. Luther spoke to them as members of the
Christian congregation. His doctrine of the two "realms"
or "regiments" is meaningful only if it is seen as
counteracting, first the medieval view that bishops have
worldly power and, second, the Anabaptist attempt to govern worldly events in society according to the words of
Jesus contained in the Sermon on the Mount. Luther wrote
in a historical situation where the union of church and
state was in the process of dissolution, even though in
his time it was still too early to see the practical results of this dissolution. Irenaeus, however, found himself in quite a different situation. The merger of church
and state had in his time not yet begun. The second-cen-
tury counterpart to the sixteenth-century princes were the
intellectual elite, the Gnostics who lacked political
power but possessed the influence that writers and intellectual leaders are proud of having today.

As I said, I did not notice much of this when I
wrote my first two historical books in 1942 and 1947. The
issue of the relation of church and state was not yet as
acute in Sweden as it became in the 1960s and '70s. In
fact, it has, since then, become more acute each year.
In today's new situation Irenaeus and Luther have come
alive to me in a new way. The attitude of the Swedish
church to the people is growing more reminiscent of the
second century than of the sixteenth. The established
Lutheran church in Sweden is losing its unique central
position as an official state-church. Moreover, active,
committed worshippers are becoming a minority among the
people as at the time of Constantine the Great.

I belong to those who are of the opinion that the

church should affirm this development and calmly assume
its new role. There is, however, conflict in Sweden
about this, just as there is conflict about the ordination of women; and I confinually take part in these con-
flicts with contributions to both battles. Taking a position in the debate about church and state has sharpened
my perception of the weaknesses of traditional state-
church Lutheranism. At the same time my respect for the
way in which the early church mastered the minority situation before A.D. 300 has grown. For the remarkable thing
about the early church settlement is that it was made at
the very time that a creed which stressed Creation first
was constructed. In the midst of martyrdom the church
held fast to the assurance that God is the God of the
whole world.

During these last years I have often heard it said
that Gustaf Wingren has become less and less Lutheran and
more and more Irenaean.[7] This is probably a correct observation, though I should like to express the matter in the
following way: I have become more and more convinced that
the person Martin Luther is a stranger to the Lutheranism
that has later, in state-church form, usurped his name.
As a theologian Luther is himself a "minority" whose work,
in a way, came too early. The Lutheran church even encouraged medieval ideas to flourish after Luther's time, since
it became the church of the state itself. This can be
seen in the spheres of church discipline, matrimonial law,
and devotional literature.[8]

I intend, with this long introduction to the
characteristically Swedish situation, to show that my
authorship began with books that are basically historical,
that is to say, descriptions of something in the past. I
treated this as fully as I do so that readers outside
Sweden can understand the profoundly relevant contemporary

meaning of what great men have thought in ages past. My
early works are historical but my choice of material,
namely the works of Irenaeus and Luther, was guided by a
modern situation of immediate importance to theology.
Moreover, from the beginning I intended the perspective
with which I chose to write both books, namely, the First
Article of the Creed, to wield a death-blow to the one-
sidedly Christological and ecclesiological theology which
is dominant today. As a matter of fact, I bear the prevailing theology of the twentieth century as an enemy
within myself. But I collect my weapons of attack by
going back to a very old arsenal.

When I wrote my two historical books I did not know
that I would spend the summer of 1947 at the University
of Basel as Karl Barth's replacement. If anyone had told
me then that in a few years' time I would be facing
Barth's international seminar composed of students from
ten nations, and that I would be trying to get this re-
sistant audience to understand the First Article of the
Creed in the face of Barth's one-sidedly Christological
criticism, I would surely have burst out laughing. Yet
that was exactly what happened. In the summer of 1947,
at the same time that the Lutheran World Federation, under
Nygren's leadership, was being founded in Lund, I found
myself in Basel. It was a boiling hot summer, both physically and spiritually. At that time, I knew nothing of
my coming Swiss adventures.

At Basel a purely historical investigation carried
no weight as an argument. At Lund, in contrast, historical material, correct descriptions, and internal analysis
of material were the marks of a first-class argument, one
superior to every other kind of argumentation. I wrote
quite a bit while I was in Lund, and in order to give an
account of what I wrote and why I wrote it, I find it best

to describe the whole of this period of authorship with
the heading "Before Basel."

II. BEFORE BASEL

Salvation means Becoming Human Again (Irenaeus)

For several reasons it is sensible to start with
Irenaeus rather than with Luther. When the reformers
started their clearing operations in the sixteenth century,
some things were so self-evident that they simply were not
questioned. One of these unquestioned assumptions was the
idea that the Bible has two parts: an old and a new "testament." Another self-evident idea was that of a Creed with
three parts: a confession about the Father, about the Son,
and about the Holy Ghost. At the beginning of the second
century, however, these assumptions did not yet exist.
The church, for example, could have chosen to arrange its
Holy Scriptures in some other way—for instance, with the
Gospels first. The church could also have chosen to give
its creed a different form—for instance, with the confession concerning Jesus Christ (now the Second Article)
coming first. Indeed, Oscar Cullmann judges this possibility to be most reasonable and most in keeping with
primitive Christianity.[9]

This did not, however, take place. The Scriptures
were arranged so that the Old Testament (with the Creation
story at the beginning) was placed before the Gospels. The
Creed was arranged in exactly the same way, with the confession concerning the Father before the confession concerning the Son. Moreover, only one thing was uttered
concerning the Father, and that with great emphasis: he
is "Maker of heaven and earth."

All contributions to the arranging of the church
order and texts of the church are anonymous. We do not

know the names of those who formed the structure of the
canon of Scripture or the Creed. However, what we can
say with certainty is that in both cases these structures
comport, even to the smallest detail, with the overall
perspective of Irenaeus of Lyons. Before going into the
doctrine of *recapitulation* in Irenaeus, however, I would
like to mention a few elementary characteristics of the
situation in which the early church found it necessary to
construct a Bible with two testaments and a Creed with
three Articles.[10]

If you were to pick up an ordinary Bible, you would
notice at once that the greater part of this book consists
of an Old Testament text. We have grown so accustomed to
the appearance of the Bible that we are no longer surprised at its irregular division. If we were to see the
book for the first time, however, we would probably be
amazed at the great number of laws about sacrifice,
slaughter, food, and the appearance of buildings, as well
as at the many stories about wars, murder, ravaging, and
about sexual crimes—all texts that are of no consequence
whatsoever for Christianity. And then, at the end of the
Bible, you would notice a few thin books about Jesus and
about little congregations scattered throughout the Roman
empire.

Now, we have become accustomed to this: we are no
longer amazed. We let the Old Testament lie there practically unused, and we begin, instead, according to in-
veterate habit, with the Gospels and Christ. We assume
that the whole book exists for the sake of this last part.

It can, however, be a good thing to experience
amazement once in a while, for we make discoveries when
we are surprised. Let us go on being surprised for a
while and thus discover some important things. For example, it is not indicated anywhere in any Old Testament

book that the text in question belongs to the Old Testament. The term "Old Testament" was not initially affixed
to the biblical Hebrew text, but was externally imposed
upon it by the Christian church. The same Hebrew text
exists in the Jewish synagogue to this day. But there
it is not called "The Old Testament": there is no reason
to speak of any "Old" Testament in the synagogue.

The long Hebrew part of the Bible cannot be viewed
as "old" until something entirely different has been added to it, something "new." This "new" part, which is
new insofar as it is written in another language, may be
short and thin. Nevertheless, it still possesses in itself a new, creative power. For the new allows us to say
that the One for whom the old Israel was waiting has in
fact come; He has been born. Because of this the Old
Testament is called "old." Furthermore, now there can
also be a "New" Testament.

Our surprise takes us further. The term "testament"
is not to be found in the biblical text. No single New
Testament writer says about himself: "I am writing a new
testament." Rather, the Christian church later externally applied this label to the text. From the beginning,
then, there were two texts, one in Hebrew and one in
Greek. Neither of these two, however, was initially
called a "testament." It was, instead, the Christian
church that decided, some time during the second century,
to put these two texts together into one book, and to at-
tach the two labels "The Old Testament" and "The New Testament" to them.

But, of course, the Christian church had given
thought to the matter and had good reasons for these
designations. The term "testamentum" in Latin and means
"covenant"; the equivalent in Greek is "diatheke." And
of course scripture speaks of God as making a covenant

with his people, both an old covenant and a new covenant
(Jer. 31:31, I Cor. 11:25, II Cor. 3,6, and 14). If we
look these passages up in the Bible, we find the word
"covenant" and we notice at once that we cannot substi-
tute the word "testament." Moreover, we also see that
we are dealing with acts of God and not with titles of
books. But it was exactly from verses like these that
the second century Christian church took its labels "The
Old Testament" and "The New Testament." Indeed, it must
be remembered that it was the Christian church that
adopted the labels. To us today "testament" means a
kind of book, a book of which there are two in scripture.
But that was not so in the beginning.

Our discoveries can be multiplied. In the New
Testament text we often find mention of "the scripture"
or "the scriptures." But never are the expressions "the
scripture" or "the scriptures" used about any text in the
New Testament. Every time that the term "scripture" is
mentioned an Old Testament text is intended, never a New
Testament text. The written book that existed for Jesus
and for the first Christian congregation was unqualified-
ly one book, the holy book of the old Israel—there was
no other. It is true that there were, in addition to
this book, oral narratives about what Jesus had done or
about what people had done to him as he was silent (during
the sentence and the crucifixion). The first Christian
congregations also had the epistles of St. Paul, which
were extant long before the four Gospels.

But in all that was new and a living word for the
world, the titles "The New Testament" and "The Old Testament" were unknown. There was only one scripture, the
scripture of Israel. Beyond that was a fulfillment of
all that the old scripture had promised: a living word
spoken to the world—the Gospel—a word which was Jesus

Christ. He arose from the dead and walked from town to
town; he walked the surface of the earth speaking life-
giving words which made everything new—words which made
the holy book of Israel "old."

The conception which underlay the formation of
these two labels remains a mystery to us. However, we
do not know who conceived the idea: possibly the origina-
tor was an anonymous theologian who lived along the coast
of the Mediterranean during the second century. But then,
we don't know the name of the man who invented the wheel
either. Some thoughts strike like lightning, under the
light of its flash; everything else arranges itself with
incredible ease. The cart, for example, simply begins
rolling. Or the Scriptures divide themselves into two
testaments, hence becoming in one sense enemies of each
other and yet belonging together. With the help of the
wheel and cart many transport problems were solved. Likewise, with the help of two testaments in a single book,
the most difficult battles the young Christian church
faced on two frontiers were resolved.

Indeed, there really were two battle lines. On the
one hand were Marcion and the Gnostics, who asserted that
the Creator was evil and Jesus good. On the other were
the synagogue and Jews, who claimed that the Creator was
good and that he had not yet sent his Messiah into the
world. To the latter the Christian Gospel was evil and
false.

The Christian community had to be able to argue on
both of these lines. Therefore, in the second century,
two excellent weapons came into being. The first weapon
was the formation of two testaments. The second was the
Trinitarian Creed.

When the two testaments were first put into one
book, the combination consisted of two incompatible texts.

This incompatibility is clearly revealed if one considers the great collections of Old Testament laws and how the early church responded to them. For the first Christian congregation could not simply neglect these laws. Yet quite clearly it was forbidden to obey them (Gal. 5:1-4). That is, what God had commanded in the old covenant—for example, circumcision—was now forbidden in the new covenant. But stranger still is the fact that the new really only comes after the death of Jesus on the cross.

Jesus himself was circumcised in keeping with the custom of that day (Lk. 2:21). His twelve Jewish disciples, a counterpart to the twelve tribes of Israel, were also circumcised. At that time his world mission had not yet begun. Only after his death and resurrection was the word of the Gospel preached to the heathen nations. For only then had what was completely new in relation to the old covenant been created (Eph. 2:15). (The new is created by an execution that takes place according to the law, followed by a resurrection from the dead, through which the executed man is enabled to step forward with the Gospel of the remission of sins against the law. The resurrection is thus the Gospel's victory over everything old.) At that point the world mission began.

Since the break between the Gospel of Jesus and the sovereignty of old Israel's law was so radical, the young Christian church fell heir to a difficult book to work with. Behind the line opposed to the Jewish synagogue it was perhaps sufficient to preach the Gospel: The Messiah has come, God's own people crucified him, and now he lives on throughout the world. But on the front opposed to Marcion and the Gnostics, it was not enough just to preach the Gospel: the Gnostics themselves preached Jesus' Gospel. But they preached it as the message of a "wholly

other God," who was elevated above the cruel laws and
wars of the Old Testament. Then in complete harmony with
this message they eliminated the idea of the creation of
the world and the body. This move had dire consequences
for the Gospel. Jesus had considered the bodies of men
worthy of healing while he had been on earth, whereas
the heavenly Jesus of the Gnostics held all human bodies
in contempt. Jesus had performed the act of new Creation
among his people, the act of forgiving their transgres-
sions against the law. The exalted savior of the Gnostics did not even struggle against the law, but was instead aristocratically above all laws. Jesus had promised
the whole human being salvation, body and soul, in the
future Kingdom of God; the Jesus of the Gnostics did not
want to bring about anything more than the invisible
soul's liberation from its soiled bodily covering. In order to keep the Gospel from being corrupted by the Gnostic
heresy, the second century Christian church was forced to
keep the Old Testament in its holy book. Their argument
against the Gnostics went thus: the Creator of the earth
and the body performed a uniquely new action through the
death and resurrection of Jesus Christ.

        The genius of this approach and of the idea of two
testaments lay in the fact that the argument against the
Gnostics was exactly the same as that against the synagogue and Judaism. The preachers of the Gospel could also turn toward Judaism and argue that the Creator of the
earth and of the body performs a uniquely new action
through the death and resurrection of Jesus Christ. Moreover, the three articles of the Creed also played this
role on both of these fronts: the Father who creates also
sends the Son, who dies and rises again and builds his
church in the world through the Holy Ghost. This congregation is the beginning of the resurrection of the dead

and of life everlasting.

   In the early centuries of the church both the idea
of two testaments and that of three articles possessed
simplicity and clarity. Therefore they also had tremendous impact. But, unfortunately, they became the church's
rule of faith, a situation which still exists today in
all confessional traditions the world over. The testaments and articles that were the result of the early
church's struggle against the Gnostics and the Jewish
synagogue have thus remained authoritative documents within the Christian church. But the enemies which made these
documents fully understandable are no longer the church's
greatest enemies. Hence, for us the Bible and the trinitarian creed are entities whose structures are difficult
to interpret.

   In such a situation it is important to maintain that
the trinitarian creed is a summary of the Biblical content
as a whole. That is why, for example, the order of the
Creed follows that of the Bible: Creation is first and the
resurrection of the dead is last. This sequence is the
natural one since the Bible begins with Genesis and ends
with Revelation. If the New Testament had been the beginning of the Bible, no one would have thought of placing an
article concerning Creation and the Father at the beginning
of the creed. The whole New Testament text is oriented
toward emphasizing the difference between the Gospels and
the faith and legalistic religion of the old Israel.
Therefore, the Second Article about Christ, who had already been born and rejected as Messiah by Israel, naturally became dominant and eventually emerged as the central
part of the creed. Note that there was no necessity for a
difference of opinion between Israel and the first Christian congregation on the doctrine of the Father and Creation. The First Article about the Creator was only later

developed polemically against the church's second century
enemy, the Gnostics, who rejected all of the Old Testament.

Therefore the First Article is, in its very formulation, an emphatic affirmation of the first and crucial
sentence of the Old Testament: "In the beginning God created the heavens and the earth." In the same way we can
see in the Second Article the outline of the Gospels.
And similarly, each of the four Gospels has the same particular structure as the Second Article. The course of
Jesus' life is described; events in it are presented one
by one. Then, the unprecedented importance of this human
life is given its character by the concluding sections
concerning the death and resurrection of Jesus, events
which occurred in fewer than three days, and yet are described in detail by each evangelist. These events acquire their supreme significance in the succession of
verbs of the Second Article: "suffered," "crucified,"
"dead," "buried," "rose," "ascended," and "shall come to
judge."

The structure of the Third Article is also, in its
own way, equally remarkable. It begins where the four
Gospels end, that is, with the first Pentecost, the out-
pouring of the Holy Ghost, and the birth and subsequent
growth of the church over the whole world. This Article
shows that the preaching of the remission of sins to all
people (Lk. 24:47) develops into an awaiting of the Kingdom of God (cf. Acts 17:31). The material for this Article comes from the Acts, the Epistles, and Revelation.

These three Articles, then, circumscribe the whole
immense content of the Bible from the very first utter-
ance, "In the beginning God created," to the last prayer,
"Even so, come, Lord Jesus." The cry for the completion
things, "Marana tá," was a mark of the early Christian of all

worship service and constituted the climate in which the
different texts of the two testaments and three Articles
were slowly assembled and given form (see I Cor. 16:22
and Rev. 22:20).

When the biblical texts are preached today, it is
therefore a long series of divine acts in the world which
is preached. God has created the heavens and the earth;
he has created all of the earth's people; he is always
near his Creation: these truths and all that they imply
are included in that series. What God did with his people
Israel, what he demanded of them, and what he now demands
of us—these, too, are included. Moreover, the whole net-
work of brotherly relations and our responsibility for
them—what one can summarize in an expression such as
"Creation and Law"—is also included in that series.
It constitutes our situation now, today: a situation in
which we find ourselves when the preaching of the Gospel
takes place for us and the church is being thereby built
up. Gospel and Church are the natural continuations of
Creation and Law.

Since this is so, the concepts "Creation," "Law,"
"Gospel," and "Church," in that order, are the most appropriate building stones for the construction of a Christian
dogmatics. This is why I first wrote *Creation and Law*
(Swedish, 1958), and then *Gospel and Church* (Swedish,
1960). They were actually written as a single book, although for publication purposes they were printed as two
separate works. I shall later come back to these books.
I would like to point out at this juncture, however, that
this dogmatic construction has deep roots in my "before
Basel" historical works, especially the one on Irenaeus.[11]
In order to better understand this connection, let us take
a closer look at the thought of Irenaeus. This
second century theologian views the work of salvation

as the restoration of a wounded humanity, that is, as
recapitulation. Salvation means that the human being
again becomes truly human. Several theologians today
direct strong criticism against this view, a criticism
that directly affects one's understanding of the First
Article of the Creed. One such theologian is Jürgen
Moltmann.[12] According to Moltmann, salvation is essentially a category of the future; therefore man opens up
to it in hope. Evidently Moltmann is of the impression
that hope would die and lose its function in the Christian life if salvation were conceived of as restoration
or the healing of something wounded. Moltmann directs
his criticism of this concept at the little word "again"
and at the prefix "re" in the term "restoration."

     Moltmann's critical attitude is grounded in the fact
that the idea of Creation has in modern times often been
used as support for reactionary political ideas. For example, the natural law theory of Roman Catholicism has
supplied arguments for conservative theories of private
property as a divine ordinance and has, in certain countries, undoubtedly hindered reasonable land reforms.
Again, during the 1950s the German theology of "Orders of
Creation" was a weapon used to sanction the established
order, whereby it contributed to a legitimation of tyranny.
It is true that these distortions of faith in the Creator
have occurred. However, an equally incorrect assumption
underlies their rejection, namely, that God created once
and for all, that today there is a created order and,
finally, that our task is to preserve this completed
work of creation.

     If Irenaeus could respond to this train of thought,
he would point out that faith in a God who is even now
Creator is being denied. Indeed, the Irenaean position
could be formulated in the following way: if it were pos-

sible for man to return to a past condition, then it
would be quite impossible to have a God who is Creator
even now. To believe in the Creator means to believe in
a God who, according to his nature, cannot do otherwise
than to create constantly anew.[13] I should add that from
one perspective this thesis fits into a mythological pattern which seems strange to modern man. This idea of
continual creation is fundamental to Irenaeus' concept of
salvation. Man is created as a child, he says, and a
child is destined to grow into adulthood. Yet, when
a child grows he remains the same person all along, even
when new things continually appear, such as the abilities
to speak and walk. Thus, though the child changes as he
grows, he yet remains the same.

Such a growing child is subject to injury and can
thereby be hindered in his movement forward toward the
goal given with his creation. Or perhaps he cannot walk
or can hardly speak. To heal such an injured or handi-
capped child may mean giving him something that he has
never had before. So, when the child's original health
is restored or recapitulated, he is *more* than he was in
the beginning and yet he is precisely *re*stored to the
sound starting-point.

The story of Adam's fall (Gen. 3:1-19) tells how
the wound got into the body of humanity. How the wound
is healed is told in the many texts about the temptations
of Christ in the desert and on the cross (Mt. 4:1-10 and
27:11-50). Through the resurrection of Christ comes the
victory of life over death, the reverse of what happened
in Adam's defeat (see Gen. 2:17 and 3:19). But the life
that Christ wins is more than the life that Adam lost.
For Adam could die; he had to grow into the state of
living forever. But Christ can never die; he lives eternally (Phil. 2:5-11). Christ is Adam—fullgrown, healthy

and whole.[14]

The Christian church with its Gospel, its Baptism, and its Holy Communion is the spring from which all people may drink of the clear water of salvation. But salvation is nothing other than becoming man—that is, being healed of the wound of sin.

Salvation, then, is restoration or recapitulation. But Moltmann, in critizing the use of the prefix "re," makes assumptions that are alien to the thought of the Church Fathers—assumptions which actually entail the denial of Creation faith. Specifically, Moltmann's assumptions exclude the possibility of reference to the Creator in speech about Creation. The point worth noting about the deteriorated modern idea of creation is its insistence on the fundamental unchangeability of the created work. God is thought of as having been Creator at some point in the past but he is not thought of as being the Creator now. While there are good reasons for Moltmann's criticizing such a distorted concept of the Creation, it is important to point out that Moltmann himself loses an essential part of the Christian faith when he—because of the distortion—flees from the First Article and isolates his theology in the Second or, more precisely, in the Third Article, the Article of hope. In so doing Moltmann loses a vital part of the Gospel.

Two New Testament texts have a good deal to say about the positive meaning of "again" or "re" as an expression of the way in which the Gospel radically deals with evil. One of the texts is the story of St. Peter's denial and restoration (John 21:14-19); the other is the parable of the prodigal son (Lk. 15:11-32). The Gospel writers could have stressed the thought that the resurrected Jesus started out with new disciples, fresh and unspent. But instead, the emphasis of the texts leads one in the opposite direction:

Jesus chooses the old disciples as his instruments. Indeed, he reinstates the very disciples who had deserted
him at the execution. This is especially true of Peter's
story, for he is reassigned the task of shepherd. And in
the parable of the prodigal son the "re" quality is the
main element, strongly emphasized in the words of the
father to the elder brother: "this thy brother was dead,
and is alive again" (Lk. 15:32). The Gospel is weakened
if this "again" is eliminated.

The mythological framework of Irenaeus is, however,
a problem. "Adam," "child," "growing," "wound,", "healing,"
—these are terms which need to be translated into a language more intelligible to us. A demythologization of
this kind has already been performed vis-á-vis the New
Testament text, in Rudolf Bultmann's famous 1948 treatise,
"Kerygma and Mythos." Further, there is noticeable agreement between Bultmann and Irenaeus as to what salvation
is. For both theologians salvation is becoming man—this,
and nothing else. Indeed, Bultmann goes further than that.
His interpretation of the New Testament Gospel as a word
cried out to the hearer which illuminates the hearer's existence follows word for word Martin Heidegger's interpretation of the conscience, *das Gewissen*. That is, Bultmann
describes the new man of the Gospel with exactly the same
words used by the philosopher Heidegger to describe the
conscience.[15]

This is, it is true, recapitulation of Irenaeus, but
with a marked reduction. What Bultmann, following Heidegger, calls "the new man," is the possibility of new life
before death, here in our historical existence. It is
not, however, as in the belief of the Church Fathers, man
as resurrected from the dead. And this reduction of Bultmann's is the exact counterpart of another of his reductions in the content of the kerygma itself, that is, the

fact that Bultman believes it is impermissible to preach
the resurrection of Christ as an external fact. According to Bultman, if the resurrection is preached as an
historical fact, the preacher creates nothing but walls
and obstacles for the human liberation of the listener.
Instead, he claims, the resurrection of Christ consists,
for the people of our time, of the fact that Christ as
crucified is *preached*. The spoken word is the resurrection and the living Christ now presented to me as my own
true self. I might add that Bultmann's theology is characterized by a remarkable inner unity.[16]

What is *not* found there, however, is the First Article of Faith, a lacuna that is in effect a part of Bultman's program of interpretation of the kerygma. For what
in the New Testament is called "kerygma" or "evangelion"
is Jesus' story, one which is focused on death and resurrection and constitutes the core of the verb forms of the
Second Article, namely, "born," "suffered," "crucified,"
"dead," "buried," "rose," and "ascended." A theology
which makes the interpretation of the kerygma its task
thereby also makes the interpretation of the Second Article its task. But no Article of Faith can stand alone,
isolated from the other two. The reductionism which results from such an isolation can be observed in Bultman's
demythologization.

My criticism of this reductionism can be stated in
three words: the body disappears. Not only does the body
in the resurrection of the dead and in the resurrection
of Christ on the third day disappear, but the social body, our
connection to others, disappears as well. Salvation is
thus, for Bultmann, individualistic in principle; it is
the releasing of the individual self from the crowd, the
liberation of the individual from the masses. It is
Entweltlichung. As Karl Barth pointed out in his debate

with Bultmann, this view of life is, at bottom, only a
new version of Kierkegaard's peculiar interpretation of
what Christianity means. For Kierkegaard, contempt for
the crowd and a negative attitude towards the natural
needs and manifestations of life among ordinary people,
were essential ingredients of his attack upon the bour-
geois Christianity of his time. Moreover, Kierkegaard
was a sophisticated Pietist: his emphasis on the individual contra the crowd in a philosophical version of the
Pietist's demands for personal conversion as opposed to
the notion of "pure faith" found in orthodox Christianity.

      Many lines of thought converge at this point. In
Pietism the law is essentially a power that discloses the
sin in the heart of man. The law is not an instrument of
God's goverance of society by means of external, physical
actions. What the reformers called the "political use"
of the law has, also, as far as I can see, entirely disappeared in Bultmann, just as in Pietism. Consequently,
the Old Testament, with its overt emphasis on the physical
and its interest in the fate of the kingdoms of this earth,
almost disappears from theology. One no longer knows what
to do with typical Old Testament texts. For the salvation
of which these texts speak is concerned with delivery from
external calamity: from bondage in Egypt, for example, or
from captivity at Babel. Theologians, however, take ref-
uge in misinterpretation, finding in the texts allegorical
allusions to Christ and the salvation of the individual soul.

      Irenaeus is a corrective to this misinterpretation.
He is therefore worth listening to, even when he develops
the somewhat bizarre doctrine of the millennium as a bodily kingdom here on earth. According to Irenaeus, from
Christ issue effects that are not exclusively concerned
with "heaven" but also with the earth, our earth, the "old"

earth. On the basis of two New Testament passages, I
Cor. 15:24-28 and Rev. 20:1; 21:4, Irenaeus construes
a detailed picture of "the kingdom of the Son," as he refers to it; it is a picture which overflows with earthly
details.[17] He attaches, for example, great importance
to external welfare, harvests, and the harmonious distribution of the harvests among the people. And in spite of
its many agrarian and purely biological traits, the picture is in many respects a political picture.

     Our modern difficulty in fitting political hope for
the future of the earth into the greater and more inclu-
sive hope of an eternal kingdom after death is connected
with the fact that we have deprived ourselves of large
parts of the Bible, chiefly those which are rooted in the
Old Testament. (The doctrine of the millennium belongs
to those parts.) It should become clear to us today, as
global problems, such as destruction of the environment,
the relation between poor and rich countries, and energy
policy come to preoccupy the community, that "salvation"
in the Christian sense cannot mean the deliverance of the
individual from chaos on earth. On the contrary, in such
a situation of deterioration salvation comes to mean the
power of the Holy Ghost over chaos to form a healed world
which includes man and nature. "The creature itself also
shall be delivered from the bondage of corruption," writes
Paul in that famous chapter about "the groaning of the
creation," a phrase which in the ecological crisis of our
time has become loaded with new urgency (Rom. 8.21f).
Irenaeus and other early Church Fathers are therefore good
guides in the search for a unified view of the Old and the
New Testaments, of earth and heaven, and of body and spirit.

     The two nouns with which I have entitled these es-
says, namely Creation and Gospel, summarize this unified

view which Irenaeus helped us to attain. There will be
many opportunities to return to these two words below,
for both the debate with Barth and with Nygren may be
reduced to this formula. At this point, however, I would
like to mention, in connection with my account of Irenaeus, my relationship to Danish theology at the University of Aarhus.

Someone who studies Scandinavian theology from the
American side of the Atlantic, could easily get the impression that there has recently arisen, perhaps not until the 1970s, a cooperation between the systematic theologians in Aarhus and in Lund. In reality, however, this
cooperation is old. It began immediately after the end
of World War II, about 1945. Indeed, the cooperation with
Aarhus belongs to the period I refer to as "before Basel."
Moreover, the cooperation is, in a very marked way, related
to Irenaeus. Both Regin Prenter and K. E. Løgstrup, for
example, were interested in Irenaeus, since they considered
Grundtvig rather than Kierkegaard to be the most important
reformer in Danish church life during the nineteenth century. Significantly enough, the spiritual current which
flows through Grundtvig's hymns, books, and speeches is
Irenaeus' doctrine of salvation as recapitulation.

It was Grundtvig who translated parts of the text
Irenaeus wrote for polemical purposes against the Gnostics
in the second century, namely the *Adversus haereses,* into
Danish. And it was precisely the separation of the Gospel
from Creation and the body which was, for Grundtvig, the
most detestable part of Gnostic theology. That is why
there is an abundance of trees, birds, brooks, and other
phenomena of nature and earthly life in Grundtvig's hymns.

Both Løgstrup and Prenter belong to this typically
Danish tradition stemming from Grundtvig. On the part of
Løgstrup, however, there is an additional factor, namely

the continuous attack upon Søren Kierkegaard's idea of
Creation, an idea characterized not only by a principle
of alienation but even by one of hatred, for, according
to Kierkegaard, everything naturally good is only there
to be sacrificed.[18] Løgstrup defended a doctoral dissertation in 1942 which was philosophical but, strangely
enough, strongly centered on the meaning of the Old Testament view of life.

     Prenter presented his doctoral thesis in 1944 under
the significant title "Spiritus Creator." The dogmatics
on which Prenter worked during the following years, which
was in its entirety published in 1953,[19] had in its title
two still more typical substantives, namely "Creation" and
"Redemption." These two terms have been taken directly
from Grundtvig. But their ultimate source is Irenaeus.

     Prenter became a professor at Aarhus in 1945,
Løgstrup in 1943, and both taught there for decades. But
both have also repeatedly lectured in Lund, just as I have
lectured in Aarhus, sometimes for whole months at a time.
This naturally laid the foundation for a good relationship
with Aarhus, one which over the years had tangible effects
on my works. Danish theology has been my teacher in my efforts to revive Irenaeus.

     More recently, a pupil of Løgstrup, Ole Jensen, has
subjected the problem of the ecological crisis and environ-
mental pollution to theological analysis in a very comprehensive doctoral thesis written in German, *Theologie
zwischen Illusion und Restriktion* (München 1975). Once
again, the biblical-theological task of providing an exegesis of the Old Testament, a Christian exegesis that allows the Old Testament to have a message of its own,
is urged upon modern theology. This task, according to
Jensen, has unfortunately been neglected.[20] As the Irenaean tradition, developed by Luther and in our

time by Grundtvig, proceeds in Danish theology, it becomes
clearer and clearer where the problem lies. I have taken
up this problem in an article entitled *Skapelse och evangelium* (*Svensk teologisk kvartalskrift,* 1977, pp. 1-11),
and will treat the subject somewhat more fully below. Here,
however, in the context of my discussion of Irenaeus, I
wish to stress especially one aspect.

        In Irenaeus' text the positive interest in the First
Article of Faith is balanced by an equally strong interest
in "the last things," or eschatology. "The last things
are like the first" is the classical rule of Christian
dogmatics. And it must be so if salvation is really *recapitulation*—the return of the original life—albeit in
a fullgrown and mature state that surpasses the original
one. Where this futuristic eschatology is allowed to remain in the system, the whole of historical life and of
the individual development of free personality will contain a "not yet" dimension. As far into the future as we
can see, in the final phase of history and in the moment
of the individual's death, there is the "not yet." Something unknown is continually awaited. It is not extinc-
tion. On the contrary, it is "the resurrection of the
body, and the life everlasting." Thus it is in Irenaeus,
and thus also in Grundtvig many many centuries later.

        This means that a healthy and uninjured humanity is
not an observable reality anywhere in the world. To real
mankind belongs the resurrection of the dead. Rather,
within the framework of history mankind has been realized
at *one* point, namely in Jesus, and more precisely, in
what is human in Jesus. (What is in dogmatics called Jesus' "human nature" is the basis for all hope of a human
life on earth.) That which is human consists in the fact
that Jesus gave of himself utterly. Phil. 2:7 says that
"he emptied himself."[21] Therefore, the foundation for a

hope which cannot be quenched by anything is the fact
that precisely *this* kind of humanity is arisen and is
now everywhere on earth, present in all of the depths of
human degradation and, finally, in death.

But if modern theology makes *demythologization* an
essential task of the Christian preacher there follows
a marked inability to speak in the face of death. In
Bultmann, for example, it is apparent that humanity or
"true existence" in the eschatological sense coincides
with what, according to Heidegger's *Sein und Zeit*, is
won in decision (*Entscheidung*) *now*, in the present. True
existence is therefore, for Bultmann, a continually new
"now." This is the core of his much discussed "realized
eschatology," which he supports with many biblical passages about heaven as "near," "already arrived," and so
on. However, only minimal social interest exists in
Bultmann's theology, though it is stronger in other modern
theologians, such as those tutored by Ernst Bloch and
other interpreters of a "humanistic" Marxism. Among these
theologians "true humanity" is no longer individualistic-
ally interpreted; rather, human life is realized in a community which includes the people, the "mass" that Kierkegaard despised and Marx called "the classless society."

In both existentialism and Marxism, therefore, "true
humanity" lies within the framework of history. Without
the preaching of the Gospel, and independent of the "yes"
of faith in the Gospel, Heidegger and Marx have outlined
what "humanity" is. And I believe it is the case that
Bultmann has added nothing to the picture that
Heidegger and Marx have already given. For he
only speaks of a "realization," albeit by way of the Gospel,
of a goal that is in principle known to us all.

Now, this is a grave loss of substance for the Christian churches of our time, basically the same loss that

characterized the impact of rationalism upon Christianity
during the age of the Enlightenment. In that time, Christianity became merely a means of realizing a "humanity"
that was defined by reason. This is in fact an anti-
prophetic orientation. Today a new version of the same
course of events is happening: conservative groups are
growing in strength everywhere within church denominations.
Often these groups are of a rather naive type, though they
are "vital," as were the Revivalist movements of the nineteenth century.

There is the danger, in this movement, that a new
wedge will be driven between what is Christian and what
is human. Currently the church claims, in a mild and
tolerable way, to provide believers with a superhuman and
divine life in the salvation offered. This wedge between
what is "Christian" and what is "human" is tolerable in
theological systems that work with the model of nature
and supernature. Catholic theology, for example, uses
this possibility in different variations: nature goes
part of the way, though not all the way, to full salvation.
The wedge becomes intolerable, however, when man is viewed
as being totally without knowledge of God, when his conscience is thought of as being unable to say anything at
all about good and evil, and when only "the revelation in
Christ" is said to give insight concerning both the Law
of God and his Gospel. Now, at the end of the twentieth
century, we are again heading in this direction. Both
fundamentalism's use of the Bible and the attempts to give
new life to Karl Barth's theology tend in this direction.[22]

At this point Irenaeus' approach is more fruitful
than these modern movements on the right and on the left.
First, Irenaeus says that to be saved is to become human,
but he does not thereby identify "humanity" with already
established patterns of individuality or community for there

is a "not yet" quality in every dimension of the prevailing order. Second, his distinction between church and
world is not one based on knowledge derived from a revelation on which the church is supposed to have a monopoly. It is not, therefore, the case that people outside
the Christian faith in the present time possess a less
perfect moral insight than the church possesses. Rather,
the church is one with the whole of humanity and bears
witness to it of a human life that humbled itself and
condescended to the lowest level. The Gospel says
that only this life lived in humiliation has defeated
death and lives eternally. Third, the future gift of the
resurrection of Christ is not insight or knowledge, but
healing, that is, regained health.[23]

    This last point is important, for healing a wound
is something quite different from giving knowledge to an
ignorant person. This is so because the gift of one who
reveals something to an ignorant person is only significant to the extent that the condition of the receiver is
poor. But the gift of one who gives healing to a wounded
person is significant to the extent that the natural condition of the receiver is good. That is, if there is
healing in one single place, I can praise the unique healer and—and this is the important point—focus at the
same time on the thing restored, namely my original health.
If, on the other hand, revelation (knowledge) is given
only at one point—say, for example, in a single book—
there necessarily arises a need to focus on and elevate
the book and, consequently, to depreciate human reason.

    This elevation of the Bible and depreciation of hu-
man reason is typical of Barthian theology.[24] Barth's
convulsive attack on the Reformation doctrine of the Law
is due precisely to his need to elevate and depreciate.
Barth believes that a universal function of the Law of God,

independent of Christ, constitutes a threat to the unique
position of the Gospel, a belief which depends on his assumption that the work of Christ as savior consists of
giving unique *knowledge* to an ignorant humanity. Since
he presupposes that this is the core of "salvation," his
awareness of the fact that the reformers, especially
Luther, speak unproblematically of the Law of God as active in the whole world, even where Christ has not been
preached, leads him to draw the conclusion that in Reformation theology there is still the idea of a residual
"natural knowledge of God." According to Barth a radically Christological interpretation of "revelation," that is,
of salvation, was not achieved by the reformation.

But as long as we accept Barth's presupposition without criticism, we do not have a historically correct picture of Luther. For Luther the Law indeed rules in the
world. But precisely because it does rule in the world,
there is no *salvation* in the world. Rather man must hear
the Gospel in order to endure living on earth, freed, as
he is, from the judgment of the Law.

Faith Lives in the World (Luther)

When we now proceed from Irenaeus to Luther, we
move almost one and a half millennia forward in time.
Irenaeus lived at a time when Europe was heathen. He
therefore represents the first small penetration of Christianity into western Europe, specifically, into southern
Gaul, the most southerly part of present day France. It
was here, moreover, that an extensive and bloody persecu-
tion of Christians took place in the second century. In
contrast, Luther lived at a time when the church possessed
more land and greater riches in Europe than any individual
person. He wanted, therefore, to break to pieces this
power and to return the church to the stewardship of the
means of grace that Christ had instituted. He thus called

her back to the preaching of the Word and the proper ad-
ministration of Baptism and Holy Communion.

These changes over the course of time are the focus
of our attention when we look at what happened in the
context of church history. If, on the other hand, we regard this movement from the narrower perspective which I
must apply if I am to account for what I have written,
the picture is quite different. In order to understand
the significance of these changes between the times of
Irenaeus and Luther, as well as that of my narrower perspective, I must digress somewhat and relate some of the
details of the development of my theology.

My book on Irenaeus was written in 1946 and published in Swedish in 1947. At that time the borders between the countries of Europe were just being opened and
one could for the first time travel and buy literature.
The openness of the channels of communication which existed in 1946 was a direct contrast to the isolation of Sweden
at the time I published my doctoral thesis in 1942. An
audience west of the Atlantic can hardly imagine the
isolated way in which a country like Sweden—a country
small, neutral, and heavily armed—then lived its life.
Lund, the town in which I did my doctoral thesis, was no
exception. A brief account of a bit of the military history of Europe during the period 1939-1945 illustrates
this situation.

In the east lay Finland, which in 1940 had just
ended a war with the Soviet Union only to be drawn into
a new armed conflict in 1941 with the same enemy. The
first war ended with a Finnish defeat and the second, in
1942, seemed to be headed in the same direction. Denmark
and Norway had been occupied by German armies since April,
1940, as was the case for all nations on the coasts of
northern Europe. Sweden was surrounded by armies, and at

the universities we were more or less restricted to using
the literature we had procured for our libraries before
1939.

The 1930s had been, however, a period of theological provincialism in Sweden. Therefore, during the period before 1939 no Swedish university, either in Uppsala
or in Lund, had had any direct contact with Karl Barth.
And as far as I know Barth never visited Sweden during
his lifetime, though he visited Denmark already in the
mid 1930s. In fact, the chair in theological ethics at
the University of Copenhagen was occupied by a Barthian,
N. H. Søe, who was appointed in 1938. Since there was no
other academic textbook on the subject, his textbook on
ethics was eventually read everywhere in Denmark, Norway
and Sweden, in spite of the fact that it was received
with disapproval and pronounced criticism. (Søe's
thought is the antithesis of that of Løgstrup
and Prenter, as well as of my thought. In Søe's many books
he, with complete consistency, takes up a position contra Grundtvig, favoring theses that Kierkegaard originated.) In my opinion the great theological debate during
this time took place in Denmark rather than Sweden.

Lund, therefore, was at this time actively involved
in historical research. Doctoral candidates sat bent
over old sources: St. Thomas Aquinas, St. Augustine, Irenaeus, Luther, Calvin. The burning theological problems
of the European continent during the 1930s and early '40s
never entered the libraries of Lund. We had only an occasional glimpse of the outside world: Søe, who had lectured in Lund before his appointment, gave us one such
glimpse, reminding us that there was, out there, a theologian named Karl Barth. Another glimpse from the outside world came from the opposite direction—conservative
German Lutheranism—which ever since the nineteenth

century had had strong ties with Sweden. Paul Althaus
had lectured in Lund before 1933, before anyone was aware
of the future political consequences of his *Theologie
der Ordnungen.*   (The term had then not yet been invented,
but the defective idea of Creation was there.) By and
large, however, we remained an isolated country.

As a student I listened to both Søe, who was the
Scandinavian echo of Barth, and to Althaus, the man who
laid the foundation of the Lutheran opposition to Barth.
Both are footnoted in *Luther on Vocation* (1942). Regarding Creation, however, I reject both of their interpretations of Luther,[25] for during my own work with Luther's
writings—work I did, in part, because of the exigencies
of the political situation—it became clear to me that
both the Barthians and the conservative Lutherans entirely missed the main point of Luther's doctrine of Creation
and teachings about the Gospel. Today I find it was an
advantage that theology in Lund was so one-sidedly directed toward historical research for I was simply driven back
to the old texts without having to ask myself at every
moment what practical decisions these texts imply for our
time. I was freed, therefore, from having to choose between two false alternatives, those represented by Søe
and Althaus.

When opposite alternatives appear equally unreasonable, one often finds that the cause of their invalidity
is rooted in a presupposition upon which both are built.
So it is in this case. The common presupposition is the
focus on revelation as *knowledge.* Both positions assume
that the central concept of theology is this sort of revelation.[26]

In the Bible, however, the concept "revelation" is not
central. And neither is it so in Luther; his central concept is justification. Only if it is made clear that this

is his central concept can Luther's reasoning regarding
the Law be retained: he assumes, first of all, that the
Law cannot make man righteous before God but is nonetheless good specifically for the regulation of external
events on earth. Therefore, he can speak positively of the
Law as a moral guide without thereby restricting the fundamental thesis that only the gospel of grace in Christ makes
man righteous. This possibility is destroyed as soon as
"revelation" becomes the central theological concept.

It was after the age of Enlightenment that this shift
in focus took place: revelation—especially the question of
how much revelation—became the main problem of theology.
The background of this shift lies in the spiritual situation
described above in the section on Irenaeus. That is, the
church ostensibly knows what "man" is and has a complete
"knowledge" within itself. But the implication of denying
that we know anything "human" except as "christian"—the idea
that theology must attempt to cut down on and reduce man's
ability to "know God"—has robbed Christian preaching of
its substance.

Both Althaus and Søe belong to this tradition.
Althaus speaks of *die Ur-Offenbarung* (an original revelation)
and adds to this, secondarily, the revelation of Christ.[27]
Søe and Barth, on the other hand, speak exclusively of "the
revelation in Christ" and attack what they call "natural
theology" or a "natural knowledge of God." However, every
mention of the works of God on earth through the Law appears
to them to be a "natural theology" and therefore a threat
to the supremacy of the Gospel. For Barth the Law is the
cellar in a building whose first and most essential floor
is the Gospel. Barth's criticism of Emil Brunner's contribution to the book *Natur und Gnade* (1934) hastened Barth's
development of this position, which was forcefully articulated in book after book during the 1930s.

But his wrath was precisely what distinguished him
from his theological surroundings in Europe. This was so
because the idealistic theologians who had learned something about the moral life from Immanuel Kant were somewhat embarrassed by Luther's doctrine of the "political
use" of the law. The same was true of the Pietist theologians who knew nothing about true conversion. For
Luther describes the elementary morality of everyday life
in terms of forces that, for example, cause us to get up
in the morning and work for our family. Luther explicitly
states that "on earth" it makes no difference whether we
do what is good willingly or unwillingly: God simply *compels* us to do certain external actions. It is this very
compulsion that is important, for it is *God*—an active,
commanding God—who is working behind the most elementary
will to live. These concepts represent the culmination
of Luther's resistance to spiritualization. God created
life, to be sure. But equally important, he creates life
now and wants to support all living creatures. And if
that is so, then it must be he that is compelling us to do
good, whether willingly or unwillingly.

Although among Swedish theologians at that time there
was much knowledge of Luther, there existed little of
Barth's wrath against "natural law" or "the worldly regiment." On the contrary, silence reigned—silence and misinterpretation. Silence characterized, for example, Einar
Billing, Arvid Runestam, Ragnar Bring, and Anders Nygren.
Only Gustaf Aulén was in any real sense free from this attempt to avoid the issue which characterized the idealists
and Pietists. (I might point out that Anders Nygren was
the theologian who most vigorously wanted to separate the
Christian faith from what is generally human.)

It was my task, then, in the year 1942, to describe
Luther's doctrine of vocation, vocational life, and life

in the family. Most important, I took upon myself the
tasks of relating his doctrine about everyday work to
his belief in the Creator and showing how the fact of
Creation leads straight to the idea of the law.

There was in particular one observation that surprised me when, without concerning myself with contemporary pro
lems and with only the purpose of giving a purely historically correct picture, I went back into the historical
material. The difference between Luther and Lutheranism,
or between Luther and seventeenth century Lutheran orthodoxy, turned out to be far greater than I had ever dreamed
it was. Two circumstances and characteristics, both understandable in light of the historical situation in which
Martin Luther found himself in 1520, were especially
striking.

In the first place, Luther wished to admonish the
church concerning her power over worldly things. In fact
I am sure that he would have wanted to go much further in
this direction than the Lutheran churches later went.
Luther was of the opinion, for example, that matrimony was
a "civil" matter and that worldly authorities, not churchly, ought to assume the duty of attending to "the entering
into and annulment of matrimony." The traditional power
of the church in this field was, according to Luther,
grounded in the incorrect and biblically untenable doctrine that matrimony is a sacrament. Similarly, he wanted
to abolish the element of "bodily punishment" in church
discipline. According to Luther, church discipline should
consist of nothing more than a refusal to give the bread
and wine of Holy Communion to a person who has sinned openly. But for external reasons it was impossible to abolish
the "worldly" power of the church: in an ordinary sixteenth
century parish often only the parish priest could read and
write. Of necessity he became "the chairman of everything."

Because of this external situation, a seventeenth century
parish, as far as the power of the church was concerned,
looked like a parish in the Middle Ages. The only differences were those which resulted from the shift of
authority from the Pope to the Lutheran Confessions. The
form of church discipline, however, remained the same,
for the church continued to exercise worldly power.

When, in 1941, I saw for the first time the extent
of Luther's radicalism—a radicalism that was strangled
already in his lifetime—it occurred to me that Luther
was, in a paradoxical way, "born prematurely." Actually,
Luther is better suited for the twentieth century than
for the sixteenth.

This radicalism is clearly demonstrated by the fact
that Luther broke with almost all of the traditions that
he had been trained to follow. The slightly nostalgic
phrase "the inheritance of the fathers" used in later
Lutheranism is not to be found in Luther. On the contrary,
Luther was continually busy throwing the inheritance of
the fathers overboard. When, however, the Lutheran interpretation became the statutory order of the land by an
act of Parliament, and when father, grandfather, and
great grandfather had been Lutherans in a continuous line,
the phrase "inheritance of the fathers" acquired a holy
ring. That is, the task of preserving this "inheritance"
became the central focus of all involved.

The difference between Luther and later Lutheranism
was one of the more surprising discoveries made while
working on Luther. I will concern myself, at this point,
with some of the more substantial aspects of his theology.

Regeneration and movement were, in Luther, the very
core of the work of reformation, both in the spiritual and
in worldly "realms."[28] He is akin to Irenaeus in his approach: the deepest concern of both could be summed up in

two words: "Creation" and "Gospel." Unique to Luther,
as opposed to Irenaeus, is his intensive concentration
on "justification by faith alone" and therefore the subsequent sharp contrast of the Law to the Gospel. As
the conflict with Rome became focused on the doctrine of
justification, the main message of Luther became characterized by these two words. This formula, "Law and
Gospel," has been articulated throughout the history of
Lutheranism.

Many important facets of Luther's reformational work
are, however, lost to view if the opposition between Law
and Gospel is separated from his doctrine of Creation.[29]
"To create is perpetually to make new" (Creare est semper
novum facere). Thus Luther defined the meaning of the
term "to create."[30] This conception of the creating God
also brings with it an idea of man in the service of God
as free and therefore liberated from all rigid patterns
of action. As Luther says, the new man "institutes new
decalogues, better than those Moses gave us." Again, love
"masters all laws," he continues. Actually, the whole description of the Christian man's freedom is characterized
by this concept of sovereignty. For Luther, Christian man
is "the freest lord over everything and subject to no one."
The chief basis of this freedom is belief in God, through
whom man is freed from the attempt to please him by deeds:
through faith there is no need for such striving. The
basis of this freedom also lies in the fact that the
neighbor, the concrete neighbor beside me, is now the only
factor that is to govern the content of my actions.

Luther's remarks about our neighbor and his needs
are of the greatest importance in understanding Luther's
remarks about freedom, movement, and sovereignty. It is
often thought that in his treatise De libertate Luther
puts forward two theses that stand in opposition to one

another, namely the thesis that man is free and subject
to no one, and that man is "the most humble servant of
every man." But in reality these two theses do not nullify one another: on the contrary, they *support* one another. Whoever really lets the needs of his neighbor decide
the content of what should be done will become perfectly
sovereign. For no Christian before me has had my neighbor. I have no reason to imitate other Christians. I
"invent" new deeds not hitherto performed. This ideal of
movement and freedom is especially developed in Luther's
criticism of monastic life.[31]

The place where we meet our neighbor and his worldly needs is, above all, in our place of work. Therefore
a whole gamut of acts is subsumed under the one word
vocatio or *Beruf*. Though many actions are performed
every day, the purpose and content of these actions are
summarized in the simple command to be faithful to one's
calling.

Practically all places of work were in those days
meeting-places between individual "neighbors." There was
no large scale industry; instead, farming and handicrafts
were the two most important ways of making a living. Thus,
when Luther let the relation to the neighbor be the locus
where the Christian's creative and inventive activities
were to function, this locus could actually become open
to fresh approaches; it was possible for the whole community of that day, which was built on agriculture and
handicrafts, to be thus renewed.

But the situation soon changed with the growth of
industrialism. The low-level employee—standing at a ma-
chine, restricted to a few technical motions—had no
"neighbor" next to him. For such a worker there was no
elbow-room for freedom; there was nothing with which to
be creative and inventive. Within the guild community,

the master, journeyman, and apprentice were approximately
equally limited by established patterns and routines. Yet, at
the same time as the industrial worker became more restricted, the opposite happened for the owner of capital.
During the period of industrialization the freedom of
factory owners increased. In an industrial society, for
example, the owner of a big factory is exceptionally free
to introduce innovations that add to the profitability of
the industry.

These changes in society came about through changes
in external circumstances, economic structures, and prevailing law. Though a Lutheran has no in-principle objec-
tion to these new circumstances, the idea of "new creation and freedom" has full scope only on the personal,
individual level, a level that was entirely swept away by
the rise of large-scale industry in the nineteenth century. The natural milieu of the Lutheran idea of vocation is therefore the countryside and the small town;
it becomes paralyzed in the city. Thus, since recent European history has, on the whole, brought increasing urban-
ization and the continued depopulation of sparsely popu-
lated areas, Lutheran piety has been driven of necessity
toward political conservatism.

Such conservatism is not, however, the essence of
Luther's thought. The ideas of multiplicity and continuous change are more characteristic of his theology, as a
closer look at his doctrine of justification reveals.
Luther sees clearly that in Romans and Galatians Paul is
fighting against a works righteousness that no longer exists in Wittenberg, namely, Judaism with its demand for
circumcision and obedience to the rules concerning clean
and unclean food, and so on. Yet Luther consciously uses
the words of Paul in condemning phenomena that did not exist in Paul's own times, for example, monastic vows and

the institution of the confessional. According to his
example, then, the content of the Gospel can be taken
from the New Testament, but the specific picture of
legalism cannot. That is, every preacher of the Gospel
must decide on the basis of his own times what works-
righteousness is. It is in preaching the Gospel that we
discover what it is in our own time that opposes the Gospel. Every age has its own form of works-righteousness
and must wage its own war against the tyranny of the Law.

The enemy against which Paul fought appeared in a
different form in the sixteenth century: the "law" is a
devil who continually changes his attire. The problem
of the changing forms of legalism is a serious one for
Lutheranism, whose preachers have seldom given clear expression to it. Today it is necessary to raise the question of whether the factory worker in industrial society
has not met the tyranny of the Law in a form unknown in
the sixteenth century, as well as the question of whether
the church was able to expose it when it appeared.[32] It
can rightly be said that in the sixteenth century Luther
placed the struggle of faith in the midst of everyday
life and assigned to Christian preaching the task of help-
ing people to achieve freedom and sovereignty in the
world. But little by little, as evangelical churches
have accepted modern technological society, which is built
on competition, Christian people have in practice uncritically drifted into a form of life that is in reality a
new legalism that worships achievements. Thus, in Sweden,
the specifically Christian has been limited to a diaconal
commiseration with "the defeated who cannot go on." Through
this development, however, the Lutheran approach itself has
been lost. The fact of this loss was connected with the
purely external changes which resulted from the state-church
system: the church lives its life as a part of the estab-

lished community and promotes conformist attitudes in
its members—the original element of protest has been
lost.

God is at work when man himself breathes, eats,
drinks, and so on. These elementary acts of life take
place among all people irrespective of whether they have
heard the Gospel preached or not. Moreover, nearly everyone in some way, in his or her own surroundings, helps such
acts of life to be performed; this help constitutes a
"morality" that is prior to any moral decision. Common-
ly, however, theologians who wish to make the Gospel of
Christ the only source of ethical knowledge leave this
out of consideration and concentrate all their attention
instead on problematic points of human behavior. Hence,
for them, God cannot be thought of as acting and present
unless his presence means the communication of knowledge,
or "revelation." The Creation faith of Luther and Irenaeus is a necessary antidote to this post-Enlightenment
view of God's revelation.

Actually, however, the approach of Irenaeus and
Luther is more "spiritual" than even the preaching of
Jesus was. For Jesus it is important, in thinking about
"God," to start with things that happen daily *without* out
associating them with God. A father gives his son a
piece of bread (Mt. 7.9f). The sun rises and the rain
falls (Mt. 5.45). A grain of wheat decays in the earth
(John 12.24). Some of these things take place among people; other things happen in the fields and pastures; others again in the animal world (Mt. 6.26). But it is *God*
who acts in what happens, and the effects of his works
are the same over this whole gamut of things, namely *life*.

This is the starting-point of Irenaeus' and Luther's
descriptions of the acts of God. They do not begin by
giving an account of the meaning of the term "revelation."

In this respect they are both deeply rooted in the Bible.
To clutter Christian talk about God with the idea that
"revelation" is the fundamental concept is typical of
theology after the Enlightenment—not of classical, biblical theology.

Neither in Irenaeus nor in Luther, however, do the
words about the Creator make the words about Jesus Christ
and salvation unnecessary. On the contrary, it is difficult to find more radically Christocentric preaching anywhere in church history than in Irenaeus and Luther. Yet
in neither is the absence of knowledge the malady under
which mankind suffers which Jesus heals. In Irenaeus mankind is dying; in Luther mankind is burdened with guilt
and condemned. It follows, then, that Irenaeus sees the
whole of salvation as centered in the resurrection of
Christ and that Luther in a similar manner sees the whole
of salvation in *justification by faith*. Neither of the
two considers the absence of knowledge concerning the will
of God a necessary condition for the preaching of the Gospel to appear meaningful. Therefore both Irenaeus and
Luther can without restraint speak of God as active everywhere.

According to Irenaeus, however much life God gives
in the struggle against death everywhere in nature, he
gives resurrection and eternal life only through one,
namely Jesus Christ, in the unique Easter event. For
Luther, however, God governs and rules through the Law in
the struggle against sin all over the world, he justifies
the sinner by one word only—the unique word of the preaching of the Gospel in which Jesus Christ lives. The uniqueness of salvation is not diminished in the slightest by the
fact that God is acting all around us. The peculiar
"stinginess" characteristic of modern theology's idea of
"revelation"—the idea that revelation is located in one

place and unknown in every other—is something from which
we cannot be freed as long as we move from one post-Enlightenment theologian to another. Instead, we must go
back behind the Enlightenment and revive theological
openness and freedom from earlier periods.

It goes without saying that the modern identification of the Gospel with a certain noetic content on which
the church has a monopoly necessarily leads to a narrow-
ing of the church. The word about Jesus Christ, that is,
the Gospel, is preached by the Christian congregation, and
is specific to the church. And as soon as it is preached
and received in faith, a church comes into existence. But
if this unique word located in the church is the only
point where God meets man, a nihilistic view of the world
outside the church and an overrating of the Christian
faith as the only basis of morality on earth necessarily
follow.

The damage of this distorted view, which deviates
flagrantly from the way in which the Gospel speaks of human life as filled with the presence of God, was felt with
great intensity by Dietrich Bonhoeffer. His negative description of the church and of her *Offenbarungspositivismus*,
together with his positive pronouncements concerning "a
world come of age," are a response to the distortion created by an unreasonable accentuation of the Gospel as a
source of knowledge for all morality.[33] But since Bonhoeffer did not have the opportunity to reach back beyond
the Enlightenment through many years of historical studies,
his later writings could only be little more than critical
aphorisms and suggestions. It is, however, of the greatest
interest that Bonhoeffer professed to prefer reading the
Old Testament rather than the New for edification. He was
looking for belief in Creation.[34]

Toward the end of his life Bonhoeffer had close, hard

contact with grim reality. During that time he had little contact with texts and libraries. In sheltered Lund
it was rather the opposite. We had little contact with
reality—in any case, little contact with the reality
that Hitler offered his people—but unlimited opportunity
for long, undisturbed work with old texts. Today I find
it to have been an advantage that the scientific surrounding a young Swedish systematic theologian in the 1940s was
as one-sidedly determined by historical research as it was.
Because of this milieu I was driven back to untainted old
sources that antedate the Enlightenment. I doubt that a
systematic theologian in any country other than Sweden
could have spent ten years of his life writing two purely
historical works on Irenaeus and Luther.

    Lund and Sweden were a limitation, but a good limi-
tation—indeed, very good for someone who was soon to go
to Basel.

    When an exegete enters into a debate in which syste-
maticians are discussing among themselves, he will often
be seized alternatively by feelings of inferiority and
feelings of superiority. When the systematicians speak
of the interpretation of biblical passages with very little
expert knowledge, it is natural for him to feel superior.
On the other hand, their biblical interpretation takes place
in a context oriented towards preaching, something
which exegetes usually do not handle; hence, the exegete's
feeling of uncertainty and inferiority.

    A young, historically inclined systematician from
Sweden might feel somewhat like that upon entering, soon
after the end of World War II, the ranks of the continental
systematic theologians in Switzerland and Western Germany.
True, these continental theologians spoke unceasingly about
Luther. Indeed, the approach of the Reformation was a direct part of both the programs of Barth's and Bultmann's

pupils. But not a single one of them was himself generally occupied with primary research on Luther, a field
which can be mastered only after several years of hard
work. Not even Barth had done primary research on Luther.
The same was true concerning Irenaeus: many spoke of him,
but hardly anyone had read him word-by-word in the original sources.

Continental systematic theology is pursued by persons who are well acquainted with the theology and philosophy of the last 200 years but who have only secondhand
knowledge of earlier periods. Their knowledge is not acquired by study of the complicated original sources, but
is instead attained through textbooks and other secondary
literature. A person who has done research on Irenaeus
and Luther feels something like an exegete: alternately
superior and inferior; more familiar with the texts than
others, but awkward, clumsy, and inferior as regards the
more extensive perspectives of Heidegger, Kant, Marxism,
Neo-Thomism, and so on.

If, however, the problem concerns belief in the Creator, the situation has a more serious side. Theology on
the Continent during the '40s moved, and still moves today,
within a sphere and spiritual climate that was formed by
specific post-Enlightenment developments. That is, Continental developments are dependent on a period in which
Creation faith was lost. The Danish theologian Ole Jensen,
whose *Theologie zwischen Illusion und Restriktion* I have
already mentioned, has described this situation. He shows
how theology after Immanuel Kant has severed the connection
between God and nature. Jensen, we recall, is a pupil of
K. E. Løgstrup and belongs to the Danish tradition that
stems from Grundtvig.[35]

I should like to present here a short account of
Jensen's main argument. The fundamental terms and key

words in the title of his *Theologie* are "illusion" and
"restriction." He gives the label "theology of illusion"
to a theology which talks about God as active in nature
in a direct and unproblematic way. According to this
sort of theology, Creation is a historical event, just as
is everything else that God has done.

In prescientific times all scholars—physicists and
chemists, botanists and historians—talked about God.
Kant, however, brought such talk to an abrupt halt. God
was banished from the domain of theoretical reason. Only
through talk about morality and practical reason could
one arrive at talk about God. Thus, human "history" became the
only context in which the term "God" found its use. Theology thereupon settled for what Jensen calls "restriction."
Talk about God was detached from nature around us.

"Restriction" was a gain, Jensen maintains. By exe-
cuting a firm retreat from nature, the theologian gained
the possibility of talking about God without falling into
the illusion in terms of which the older, prescientific,
seventeenth century theologian thought. Today, we recognize the nineteenth century way of thinking and consider
it self-evident. The disciplines (geology, botany, physics,
chemistry, and other exact sciences) are concerned with nature around us; to bring God-talk into the picture is un-
thinkable. But there still exist some independent questions of another sort, namely ethical and religious ones.
These questions are nonscientific but nonetheless necessary
and with them appears again, suddenly and acceptably, all
the discarded God-talk. Theologians here find a place to
live. But in this place it is possible to deal only with
man; animals, plants, trees, wind, air and sunshine lie
outside of it.

"Restriction" is a gain, but, according to Jensen,
the resulting loss of theological content was too high a

price to pay. It will take centuries to make up the
losses. Today we are suffering the consequences of this
exorbitant price: the ecological crisis—the destruction
of the environment and the defilement of nature—has made
us aware that something is wrong in the nineteenth century model of thought.

    It is interesting to observe how what we have called
"science" since Kant has become laden with values, albeit
certain sorts of values, which all stand in an *exploitative*
relationship to nature. Science has not excluded values;
it has only denied some, namely those which allow for the
respect of nature, reverence, gratitude, and gladness for
nature's beauty, and so on. Such values are supposedly
unscientific and must be excluded from serious and exact
scholarship. Values relating to the utilization and exploitation of the environment are, however, acceptable to
the scientist and are freely and casually built into the
new sciences which are being added to the older university
disciplines. What unites the old and the new is exactness
in method and measurable results.

    A forest can be described scientifically. Every
tree can be examined and its qualities, hardness, and usefulness for construction can be assessed. If one views
the forest, for example, as a potential supplier of wood-
pulp, one can then speak, in the language of science, of
the value of the forest. There are economists in the university who do just that, and one cannot challenge the
scientific validity of their discipline.

    On the other hand, if one describes a tree as sooth-
ing to the mind, as cooling presence in the woods, and as
bringing cheer through its foliage, his perception represents a type of value which is just as securely rooted in
human needs which reflect, indeed, an even more basic human need than the economic calculation of profit. This

human need is expressed in poetry, not in scholarly research, and is based on, among others, the unscientific
values of reverence and gratitude for nature. Today,
however, even social scientists have begun to discover
these values that cannot be read directly in terms of
figures, money, and usefulness. It is enough to note
that the nineteenth century model of thought has had its
day and has exhausted its resources; yes, literally exhausted them. Nature's supply is not inexhaustible. The
value of trees for manufacturing paper is ended once the
paper pulp factories have taken them. Those who value
the coolness and freshness of the trees, on the other
hand, allow the tree to stand and do not exhaust the resources of nature. Increasingly, this latter viewpoint
has been emerging as the reasonable one.

     It is strange that such reasonable values may not
be expressed in other than poetic form, while the other,
sometimes injurious and unreasonable, values receive broad
acceptance in the scholarly world. Today, however, exact
scientific language is beginning to look stupid.

     During the nineteenth century theologians followed
the general trend and accepted the method of "restriction."
They talked about man and God without talking about a direct relation between nature and God, a relation about
which the biblical texts speak at great length. Theologians, therefore, must share the culpability of the exact sciences for the exploitative thinking which has been
dominant in the West.

     The above is a brief summary of Ole Jensen's view,
which on the surface sounds like a common current position.[36]
Jensen, however, takes it in a completely different direction.

     It is generally accepted that the theologian is
faithfully following biblical directions when he develops

the view that man is absolutely dominant vis-á-vis nature.
Jensen contends, however, that in doing so the theologian
has followed a nineteenth century, Neo-Kantian model that
contradicts the biblical texts. For the scriptures speak
of nature as God's and awaken in man reverence and respect for it. That mankind, according to the creation
story, is given a managerial task over nature does not
diminish the explicit biblical basis for the argument that
God *meets us in creation* and that he himself as God is
directly active in creation. Thus, there is no need to
take an ethical, religious path to God.

This is the problem as Ole Jensen has outlined it.
How are we as modern theologians to return to a pre-Kantian
directness in our understanding of God and nature while at
the same time avoiding the "illusion" of the seventeenth
century way of thinking, an illusion which put the events
of the history of Creation into the calendar and the time-
line of history. We must escape "restriction," the limita-
tion to mankind only, and yet we may not end up in "illusion." Hence the title of Jensen's dissertation: *Theology Between Illusion and Restriction.* In this context we
can see that Løgstrup is a model for Jensen, but only in
the sense of a beginning, or a point from which one leaves
to arrive elsewhere.

I have earlier touched upon Løgstrup's original
writings, which he began in 1942, and his influential
teaching in Aarhus for more than one generation. I will
return to contemporary Danish theology and to the questions
it raises below. I took up Ole Jensen's dissertation of
1975 at this point in order to illustrate the deadlock of
European theology in a situation whose elements are determined by problems that were brought to the forefront by
the Enlightenment. To these belong the disappearance of
Creation faith and the dominance of the concept of reve-

lation. Of course, the situation was aggravated by the
fact that it was within *theology* that Creation faith became marginal. As is well known, in politics the movement was in the other direction. National Socialism had
a great deal to say about "creation," "race and blood,"
and so on. The First Article therefore had a bad reputation for purely political reasons.

This was the situation when I came to Basel in April,
1947. Hitler had just died. The work of cleaning up was
still going on in Germany; among other things the theological faculties on which the "German Christians" and other
related groups had served were being purged. The respectable theologians had belonged to "The Confessing Church,"
which was more or less dominated by the dogmatics of Karl
Barth. All were, without exception, Christologically inclined. As a matter of course all of their theological
analyses started with the "revelation in Jesus Christ" as
the basis. To question this basis generally meant putting
oneself outside the then current theological discussion.[37]

The forte of Continental theology was, in my opinion,
quite clearly the "kerygmatic approach." This strong
point was, moreover, lacking in Swedish theology—its
greatest deficiency. Theology would never have been able
to confront National Socialism with the Swedish historicizing method. Barth's theology, in contrast, was constructed exactly to do battle with a political ideology
of the type that held sway in Germany from 1933 onward.
No church whose theologians isolate themselves in historical investigations can ever deal with current alternatives
to Christian faith. This was noticeable in the '60s when
Marxism became a widely discussed alternative. Those theologians who started with the kerygma furnished the most
valuable and fruitful contributions at that time as well.

But a kerygma is a "message from a herald" which

presupposes something quite definite about the person to whom the call is directed.[38] The kerygmatic approach presupposes a mankind that is created but has now been taken prisoner by destructive powers. This approach of the kerygma, the cry of the herald, is constantly threatened with becoming empty when the addressee is assumed to be primarily "ignorant" or "without knowledge" instead of created and fallen. For the Gospel and kerygma presuppose a human who is created by God though at enmity with him through rebellion. On the other hand, the idea of man as lacking a certain knowledge goes with the concept of "revelation." Furthermore, the Gospel becomes, in this context, a replenishment of knowledge about God. The kerygmatic strength of Continental theology since 1920— one shared by both Barth and Bultmann—does not stand in any in-principle opposition to an accentuation of the First Article of the Creed. Only the starting point of "revelation in Jesus Christ" presents such an in-principle opposition because Creation and the kerygma belong together. In other words, Creation and Gospel belong together.

What I repeatedly refer to as "Creation" and "Gospel" actually constitutes a unity in classical Christian theology. Moreover, we would be able to see this if we could rid ourselves of the fixation upon an intellectualistic concept of "revelation" to which we have become addicted after the Enlightenment. To free ourselves from this intellectualism would really be "proceeding forward," to borrow an expression used earlier within the present section. But this freedom can only be gained by consciously "making our way back" to the ancient wellspring of pre-Enlightenment biblical interpretation.

The ancient interpreters of the Bible (this is true of Irenaeus and Luther, among others) are not effective or powerful promulgators of the unity of "Creation" and

"Gospel" by virtue of their systematic argumentation
or the coherence of their "theologies." Rather, their
true strength exists entirely in the fact that they
draw attention away from themselves to the Bible texts
to which they continuously subordinate themselves. It
is in the original *biblical* word that the strongest arguments contra Karl Barth are to be found.

As an example, I shall take the relation between
God's Creation of the world and all the peoples of mankind on the one hand and God's election of the single
people of Israel on the other. For Barth, the crucial
point is that God gives the Law after the Exodus from
Egypt, that is, to a people who have first received salvation or "the Gospel." Through this perspective Barth
preserves, in spite of the Bible itself, his cherished
order of terms and events: Gospel first, then Law. This
was the main thesis of Barth's 1935 treatise *Evangelium
und Gesetz*.[39] Moreover, through this kind of argumentation accrued, at that time, a benefit to the church.
It had a "revelation" in the Gospel, so it won a morally exclusive position contra the nationalistic German state,
which in the '30s spoke of *Schöpfung* and of the majesty of
the *Herrenvolk* as rooted in "race and blood." Barth sees
the idea of Creation as spiritually risky. He does not,
however, view the belief in the "Exodus" and election of
Israel in the same way.

Yet, though he assigns greater credibility to belief
in the Exodus and election of Israel, Barth misses an important point in the biblical text, namely the prophetic criticism precisely of Israel's belief in its specific election, a criticism that should be earnestly directed against
the exclusivity of the church of the twentieth century, as
Bonhoeffer was later to realize. The Bible overflows with
texts that clearly show that nationalism and belief in

one's own people are the antithesis of faith in the Creator. It is precisely this faith that we should develop
if we want to destroy national and particularistic pride.

One simple example of this prophetic criticism is
Amos. He stood before a people who believed in their own
election and who prided themselves on their unique position among the nations of the world. Amos regarded the
isolation of one of God's acts, namely the Exodus from
Egypt, as the basis of this distortion. When he wanted
to destroy nationalism he destroyed the exclusivity of
Israel's appeal to the Exodus. For Amos God is the Creator who has led many peoples out of poverty, not just
Israel. "Are you not like the Ethiopians to me, O people
of Israel?" says the Lord. "Did I not bring up Israel
from the land of Egypt, and the Philistines from Caphtor
and the Syrians from Kir?" (Am. 9:7-8). The great death-
blow to the worship of one's own people is this very word
which says that God has created everything and now holds
the weal and woe of all mankind in his hand (Am. 9:5-6
and 5:8).

The Barthian theologians should have from the beginning taken texts of this kind as a starting point for a
biblically correct doctrine of Creation contra all nation-
alisms. Instead, however, they stressed the Exodus ideology, applying it to the church of our time, thus laying
the foundation for the ecclesiasticism that to this day
paralyzes European theology. When Creation statements
are misused, which was undoubtedly the case in the preaching of the "German Christians," there is good reason to
widen and clarify the doctrine of Creation rather than to
suppress it. Many texts which clarify the doctrine of
Creation may be found in the Bible, if such help is desired. Such material is plenteous, and one's understanding
of these biblical texts may be guided by the ancient inter-

pretaters who lived before the Enlightenment and the
Pietistic Revivalist movements.

It is fairly easy to look back and collect biblical
texts. To move forward, however, and really break through
the barriers of modern theology is difficult. The difficulties I encountered were most clearly noticeable during
the very latest years when the barriers had, to a certain
degree, begun to give way. Pupils of Barth were beginning,
though with hesitation, to say things that were not derived solely from the Second Article of the Creed and the
revelation given in Jesus Christ. The place to which they
proceeded was the *Third* Article, not the First. As an old
man, Barth himself had expressed his longing for a future
Theologie des Heiligen Geistes, a theology of the Holy
Spirit. There, under the heading of the Third Article of
Faith, he believed it would be possible in a positive way
to take up all the subjects that had been treated in the
'30s under the First Article. (In this respect the newly
published investigation of Christoph Gestrich on the history of dialectic theology is of the greatest interest.[40])

The influence of the eastern branch of the church's
tradition, long neglected in western theology, has been of
some importance on this point. After the assembly of the
World Council of Churches in New Delhi in 1961, the basic
thoughts of the Orthodox Church flowed into ecumenical
work. There is, of course, another relation among the
three Articles of the Creed in the east than the one to
which we in the west are accustomed.

In the western branch of the church, the well-known
conflict regarding the *filioque* caused the Holy Ghost to
be subordinated to the Son. In the Nicene Creed we use
the formulation "the Holy Ghost, the Lord and giver of
life, who proceedeth from the Father and the Son." The
east, on the other hand, retained the formulation "who

proceedeth from the Father." In this formulation the
Father sends forth twice; he sends the Son (Gal. 4.4),
and he sends the Spirit (Gal. 4.6). This means that the
Spirit (and thereby the Third Article of Faith) had an
entirely different and more "open" place in the east than
it had in our western tradition.[41]

According to many Old Testament passages the Father,
as Creator, works through the Spirit (Ps. 33.6 and 104.30,
see also Gen. 1.2). The eastern tradition makes room for
speaking of this activity of God in the world outside the
church with this recognition. Moreover, to place Creation
in the Third Article in this instance does *not* mean the
subordination of Creation to "revelation" as given in
Jesus Christ—a revelation which is preached by the church
alone. The Spirit in such a formulation is free and works
in all human forms of love, service, and liberation—in
all forms over the whole earth.[42] However, when Karl Barth,
who is a western theologian, speaks of the Holy Spirit he
is dependent on the traditional concept of the Spirit as
emanating from the Son (*filioque*), as Christoph Gestrich
argues in his recently published work.

Even at this late date in the '60s and '70s it is
possible to observe how tenacious the opposition against
the First Article was—and is. It seemed as if for Barth
and his school there was something intrinsically repulsive
in the word *Schöpfung* or "Creation." The themes that traditionally belonged to the First Article were disregarded
as long as it was possible to disregard them. When it
finally became impossible to suppress the problems associated with the First Article any longer, and thus when they
were pressed into the foreground so that it became impossible to avoid treating them, they were taken up under a
different heading than that of the First Article. That
is, they became treated under the rubric of the Spirit,

in the doctrine of hope, rather than that of Creation!
But in 1947, when I arrived at Basel, these "maneuvers
of suppression" were far more common than they are today.
They were   carried out with greater anger, and the effects of the maneuvers were stronger than now. Anyone
who spoke then of *Schöpfung* was viewed as a defender of
Hitler.

The theologian among the Barthians with whom it
was easiest to talk——the only one, as a matter of fact,
who admitted that Karl Barth had led Continental theology
down a blind alley by his "no" to nature and his "yes" to
the Gospel as the exclusive source of knowledge of the
good, was Hans Iwand, professor of systematic theology
at Göttingen from 1945-1952 and at Bonn from 1952-1960.
For ten years he had been forbidden to teach at German
universities (1935-1945) and proudly referred to this
muzzle imposed by the authorities as his chief qualifica-
tion. I often had long talks with him, during which he
looked back on the whole period from 1933 to 1950. (I
was a "guest professor" at Göttingen during the summer of
1950, and it was chiefly then that our conversations took
place.) Iwand was extremely outspoken when he addressed
the question of the Barthian view of church and world.

During Hitler's time Iwand had been a minister in
the Confessing Church. "It was a wonderful time," he
told me, suppressing a smile. "Then we had to explain to
Hitler what the *Church* is, and on that subject we had good
theological insight." But with respect to the period that
began with the defeat of Germany in 1945, Iwand never expressed himself with the same lightheartedness. All of
the old political authorities in Germany had fallen by
that time, and the ministers of the Confessing Church belonged to the small number of persons for whom the occupation forces had respect and who therefore were immediately

placed in positions of responsibility for the reeducation
of the German people.[43] "After 1945 we had to explain to
the people what the *world* is, and on that subject we had
no theological insight," Iwand declared, with a frankness
regarding this point that is seldom seen among the Barthians.

Iwand often expressed a deep loyalty to the Barthian
theology that had emerged in the Confessing Church in the
'30s. But this loyalty was combined with a clear understanding of the theology's weak points. Iwand saw, for example, the obvious differences between Luther and Barth and
did not wish, as for instance Ernst Wolf did, to hide this
difference.[44] What was unusual about Iwand's attitude was
the fact that he was able to assent to Barth's approach in
a historical situation determined by the phenomenon of National Socialism and, at the same time, to see with open
eyes, and openly admit, the deficiencies of Barth's approach. Iwand could therefore admit that criticism of
Barth was necessary in a new historical situation.[45] Such
admissions were, however, rare during the period that immediately followed the end of World War II.

There was no doubt in my mind that a thorough criticism of Karl Barth and his school was justified. However,
the atmosphere in European theology in 1947 made every debate into something of a drama. At the same time, the
disquieting aspects of the conflict for me personally were
heightened by the obvious deficiencies of my own training.
To a Swedish theologian with a one-sided historical orientation it was quite impossible to enter into conflict with
the strongly dialectical theology without self-criticism.
During my stay at Basel the entire Swedish system of doing
theology came to appear unsound to me in the long run. At
some point Swedish theology should have been subjected to
criticism, and the target should have been the crucial

absence of any kerygmatic approach in Sweden—an absence
which issued in paralysis and escape into the past.

It is true that I protested against Barthian theology at Basel but I was also converted to Barth
there. Both protest and conversion had consequences. I
wrote two books in the "after Basel" period. I will
herein follow the chronological order that describes the
appearance of these books in English: *Theology in Conflict* (1958) and *The Living Word* (1960).[46]

III. AFTER BASEL

An Historian Protesting

My book on preaching [*The Living Word* (1960);
Swedish (1949)] is an open one, filled with biblical material. My book on theological method [*Theology in Conflict* (1958); Swedish (1954)], on the other hand, is relatively narrow and closed, one-sidedly restricted to the
time of the Reformation and Luther.   This narrowness
is the result of the almost purely negative and polemical
exposition it directed against the three theologians who
from 1920 to 1960 dominated the debate on theological
method in Europe, namely Karl Barth, Rudolf Bultmann, and
Anders Nygren.

After World War I these three theologians began systematically to give new life to the approach of the Reformation; all three regularly call Luther's theology a
"theology of the Word." In my debate with them, therefore, I myself was necessarily restricted to the Reformation, that is, to the problem of Law and Gospel.

It is rather remarkable that it was possible, at the
beginning of the '20s, unrestrainedly to connect up with
the Reformation of the sixteenth century and, in so doing,

consider oneself progressive, radical, and critical of
the prevailing order.   In book after book Nygren, for example, asserted that Catholicism represents an "egocentric"
religion whereas Luther represents a "theocentric" one.[47]
Theocentricity had clearly become a positive value which
was then found in Luther, an assumption that in those
days aroused very few protests: Luther had not yet acquired a bad name.   Karl Barth placed himself directly
in Luther's line and gladly considered himself a person
akin, in spirit, with the end of the Middle Ages.   In fact,
he considered it an honor.[48]   In Bultmann the direct ad-
herence to Luther was delayed, but when it came, it came
in earnest, for the aim of demythologization in our time
is the same as what Luther hoped for with his doctrine of
"justification by faith."[49]

     The change of climate around 1920 was remarkable.
Most remarkable of all was the ease with which people
suddenly began to assert the opposite of what they had
quite recently said.   In order to understand this change
of climate it is necessary to acquire a (rather lengthy)
perspective on the spiritual development of Europe.   The
term "Luther" in 1920 did not stand for the whole of the
real Luther.   There had long been a peeling off of one
layer after another: Creation faith, the "civil" use of
the Law, the idea of "the secular regiment"—these important parts of the Luther corpus had either fallen by the
wayside or become rudimentary appendages lacking vitality.
There remained only the ideas of "justification by faith"
and "the Gospel alone" as the foundation of salvation.

     This reduction had taken place as early as the Re-
vivalist movements of the nineteenth century.   (It was
already, at that time, observable socially as a conscious
retreat from cultural life.)   And it is this reduced

Luther that Nygren, Barth, and Bultmann place in the center again. But they did this at the same time that they
assented to those general cultural phenomena that appeared
radical, modern, progressive, and "worldly." Barth was a
socialist; Bultmann and Nygren were adherents of critical
philosophies that sought to demolish all metaphysics.
(Heidegger and analytical philosophy share an antipathy
for metaphysics). With a certain intensity all three are
suspicious of man's own cultural possibilities. The same
suspicion characterized the Revivalists' flight from culture in the nineteenth century. This posture became dominant at the leading universities of Europe during the
1920s.

        This fact is not as paradoxical as it appears. Lib-
eral theology with its openness to the entire cultural
world had been an antidote to the narrowness of Revivalism.
But, in origin, Liberal theology was an offshoot of the
Enlightenment with its unlimited faith in the reason of
man. Liberal theology is a theology without an eschatology. Instead, it has an optimistic Creation faith which
left the Liberal embarrassed about the Bible's own view
of sin and death. Though many outward calamities could
take place without shattering this cheerful optimism, one
misfortune was unendurable. If mankind itself could wit-
tingly start a project whose only result was death and
destruction, then this optimistic Creation faith could
not survive. World War I (1914-1918) was just such a misfortune. Barth, Bultmann and Nygren came to prominence
in 1920 an altered climate.[50]

        All three spoke of Luther, but they were Christo-
logical theologians in the tradition of Revivalism, not
in the tradition of the Reformation. For by 1920 the
term "Luther" already had a reduced content: the work of

reduction had been performed by Revivalism against the
Enlightenment and its optimistic, shallow Creation faith
devoid of eschatology and any realistic view of destruction.   The Enlightenment relied on a reduced First Article of Faith and Revivalism on a reduced Second Article
of Faith. Though this sounds like caricature, it was the
actual situation around 1920.   It was at that time possible to hastily write theology that spoke negatively of
human reason and positively of the "revelation in Christ."

This theology which evaluates human reason negatively and "revelation" positively must, in the long run,
necessarily place the church in the center of the whole
system.   With the Second Article as its only base, Revivalism, for example, had resulted in the establishment
of pious groups of truly converted persons.   The great
national church, on the other hand, remained, on the
whole, unaffected by this reductionist theology, for it
included the whole population of the country and was not
composed of "the converted." By their very existence
the national churches of Europe represented a form of
Creation faith, even in those times when the Creation
faith was neither theoretically articulated nor the subject of reflection in university theology.   Parishes with
geographical boundaries are purely external arrangements,
it appears; but built into this arrangement is a profound
faith in Creation: the place of work, birth, death, matrimony—everything is encircled by the church and therefore by the Father of Jesus Christ.[51]

This situation changed about ten years after 1920.
European theology then experienced an unheard of renaissance of the doctrine of the church and ecclesiology.
Not since the Middle Ages has the concept of the church
occupied such a dominant position in theological work as

in the period after 1930. This is true among Lutherans,
Presbyterians, Catholics, and Anglicans, among others.
Of course, an important explanation of this is growing
ecumenical work, which immediately resulted in the differences and similarities of various views of the church
being placed at the center of attention. But the main
reason for the prominence of ecclesiology is to be found
somewhere else, namely in the isolation of the Second
Article of Faith.

The Reformation, I might point out, did not give
rise to any such mass of ideas about the church. Rather,
the content of the preached message of the Gospel was the
focus of discussion. Moreover, as a social phenomenon
the members of the congregation were distributed among
the many vocations of the world.

Since 1930, however, "the church" has become a theological theme in its own right. The question of the
boundaries of the church is now especially important.
But since there is no theological interpretation of
"world" or of "mankind," the environment of the church
becomes an undefined something to which the church makes
social and political "contributions." These contributions are viewed as actions required by the Gospel, that
is, by "the revelation in Jesus Christ." Furthermore,
these contributions are almost like raids into an alien
country that is theologically unknown and impossible to
describe. Only from the vantage point of the doctrine of
creation can the "territory" surrounding the church be
described, but, unfortunately, Creation faith has had
marginal existence since 1920.

If we drop theology out of the picture, then of
course the surroundings of the church can be described
perfectly well. For example, Barth can use ordinary and

conventional political terms; Bultmann, Heidegger's anthropology; and Nygren, the neo-Kantian philosophy of
the four fields of experience outside the religious area. B
Such theology *qua theology* says nothing more about these
surroundings than that which it derives from the Gospel.

This is the regrettable result of the fact that
theology has become Christology. This is so not only in
Barth, but also in Bultmann and Nygren. If we speak of
the kerygma (Bultmann) or *Agape* (Nygren), we are speaking of something specific to the New Testament and to the
Second Article of Faith, the content of which is given
through Christ. When this content is turned into the
full content of theology, however, a classical category
that was very important in early periods of church history is lost, namely "God's *new* deed in Christ." According to reformational and classical theology God is constantly at work everywhere, but he creates something entirely *new* in Christ. When Christology becomes everything, however, as it does in modern theology, this "newness" cannot be preserved. It is instead mixed up with
an entirely different kind of newness, namely with what
is new or unique in the Christian church as compared to
other world religions. The upshot of these shifts is a
radically changed situation for the concept of the Law.

In such a Christocentric theology the Law can no
longer be thought of as active in the world before and
independently of the preaching of the Gospel. For since the
Gospel, out of whose preaching the church arises, constitutes the source of the contributions the church makes in
the world, as a matter of course one seems impelled to
turn to the question of what the social principles of
"evaluation" are that lie enclosed in the Gospel. In this way
the Law's location is shifted. The Law is not thought to

be already in the world. If the Law is therefore to come
into the world, it must come from the church, from the
group that assents to "the revelation in Christ" given in
the Gospel. The Law then comes from the Gospel and *only*
from the Gospel, as Barth consistently argues.[52] Worldly
existence in itself lacks a created structure and must
thus receive its ordering structure from the church, from
the *Christengemeinde*.

Fifty years have passed since this line of reasoning was first put forth. Yet in two respects the cultural situation of today is already radically different from
the spiritual climate after World War I.

In the first place, around 1920 everyone still made
certain "Constantinian" assumptions, namely, that the
church and its preaching of the Gospel stand in the center
of the worldly community, which listens to the word it
speaks. This can be seen most clearly in the debate that
was conducted at that time about the ostensible *autonomy*
of the different areas of human life. This debate concerned the question of *Eigengesetzlichkeit,* that is, the
idea that there are autonomous spheres within society—
for example, art, economy, and politics—which are independent of one another. This debate was focused on the
question of how much autonomy each of these areas has. Inevitably "autonomy" was, in this context, conceived as
autonomy in relation to the message of the church. Today
we see clearly that these spheres limit and reduce each
other's freedom. For example, art is limited by its relation to politics, which in turn is limited by its relation to the economy, and so on. The church no longer
stands at the center of the community, limiting the autonomy of the other areas of life.[53] The Constantinian
epoch has drawn to a close.

In the second place, around 1920 everyone assumed a passive and inexhaustible biotic environment that allows man to exploit everything in total, expansive freedom. Hence, no theology counted on nature as active and able to strike back at man. Today, however, we see clearly that a polluted and exploited biotic environment constitutes a threat. The ecological crisis has opened our eyes to a reality which we have ignored despite the fact that earlier generations, which had greater respect for nature than we have, knew a good deal about it. It was also in keeping with the escapism of the Constantinian epoch that the church, standing in the center of the society and allied with its governing forces as it was, uncritically assented to profit and economic growth.[54]

Insight into the workings of this ecological crisis has grown. We realize today that round about us there are processes in progress that give us life apart from the church and its preaching, as well as processes that give us death, that is, express the wrath of the Creator, apart from the church and its judgment. If tested against these new insights, two theological positions are shown to be more untenable than they seemed around 1920. The first is an optimistic Creation faith that is blind to destruction: such optimism can no longer be maintained. And it is precisely this shallow type of Creation faith based on an isolated First Article which has, ever since the Enlightenment, been found in European Christianity: its seeds existed already before 1920 in the form of "Liberal theology." But equally untenable is a Christological dogmatics based on an isolated Second Article, as is the case in the theologies of Nygren, Barth, and Bultmann.

Many people are today realizing the significance of the ecological crisis for raising our consciousness of

creation and its antithesis, destruction. I cannot say,
however, that when I came to Basel in April 1947, I saw
the whole connection clearly. For had I seen it, I would
have structured my books differently. I saw, instead, an
historical fact. I saw that the idea of Creation that the
Christocentric theologians in Europe around 1920 unanimous-
ly criticized was an entirely modern and trivialized idea
of Creation which had its roots in the Enlightenment. All
of what was essential to the doctrine of Creation during
the struggles of the second century against the Gnostics,
the core of which was still included in the doctrine
during the sixteenth century struggle for the recognition
of ordinary, everyday work, was lost in Liberal theology.
Lost were the convictions that God is active in the whole
of human life—indeed, in all that surrounds man—and that
destruction at every point threatens what he has created.

The talk of "the Creator" and "the Creation" that
flourished in the shallow Creation faith of the first half
of this century represented, therefore, a deterioration
and lacked the strong foundation of the First Article of
faith as it was originally intended to be interpreted.
By the same token, the talk about the "revelation in Christ"
which flourished at the same time in opposition to the idea
of Creation also represented a deterioration in comparison
with the way in which the Second Article was interpreted
in the classical periods.

The growth of this opposition can be characterized in
this way: in the absence of a functioning First Article, reality around us and in us was emptied of creative and destructive powers, that is, of God and the Devil. Under
such circumstances it became a problem even to use the
word "God." Thus the incarnation came to be viewed as
that point in history where "God makes himself known" or

"shows us who he is." God and his work are thought to
be invisible except in Christ and "revelation."

The idea that God is visible only in Christ is a
theorization of the concept of revelation.[55] The biblical word for "reveal" means "to uncover." It assumes
that there exists something which has been around for a
long time but has remained concealed or hidden. What is
revealed—uncovered—may be the decree of salvation (Tit.
1:3, Rom. 1:17), the wrath of God (Rom. 1:18), or the
justice and judgments of God (Rom. 2:5). The stereotyped
formula "God has revealed Himself in Christ" is, thus,
modern and based on an assumption that is not found in
the Bible, namely, the assumption that nothing in life
indicates that life is given and is now threatened by destruction. Instead, we are thought to be surrounded by
raw matter that exists by chance and is itself passive,
only becoming something when we humans form it. God is
not there; rather we exist alongside a powerless raw material.

This is an assumption that has become more and more
common since the Enlightenment: the idea that God's existence is in no way evidenced within *our* existence.
Rather, the life of Christ is isolated and asserted to
make it probable that God exists. Thereby, what does not
appear probable on the basis of ordinary human life becomes probable at the sight of Jesus.

The term "God's revelation in Christ" is not the organizing principle of the New Testament. Likewise the
Reformation proceeds without this term as a heading over
its message. It seems then that the general domination of
the term in recent theology must be connected with the
fact that the entity "God" has generally become problematic.
But the problematic nature of our talk about God does not

soften the hard fact that "revelation" has acquired a
place in modern theology that is totally alien both to
the biblical text and to the Trinitarian Creed.

There are two differences between this way of thinking and the early church's view of life. First, what God
does in Christ is now more theoretically conceived than
it was in earlier periods. It is no longer thought that
in Christ's death and resurrection God achieved something
designed to lift man out of death and bring him into life,
that is, out of bondage and into freedom. Rather, the
supernatural contribution of knowledge from God to us via
Christ has become the main focus in modern theology. Second, the modern theologian's view of ordinary, natural
human life is more nihilistic than it was during the time
of the early church. We are born, eat and drink, receive
the sun's warmth and the night's beauty, but do not meet
God—only "life," as we now put it. But a person who
talks about what we can expect from "life," or what "life"
gives us, speaks mythically. In fact, after the Enlightenment the term "life" came to stand for a reality that in
earlier periods was called "God."

When the processes that are generally human are emptied of divine deeds and God's act of revelation is located
at a single point, that is, Jesus Christ, then, in principle, the same interpretation of life as that of the second century Gnostics is accepted. Marcion's theology, for
example, can be summed up with this thesis: God has revealed himself in Christ and only in Christ. Against just
this view of life the Apostolic Creed with its three parts
was built. The fact that the Church Fathers considered
this theology to be a greater threat to faith than Atheism
bears witness to their good judgment.[56]

Today, in the twentieth century, this concept of

revelation is again a factor which undermines faith. For
very often our basic trust and confidence in "life" must
confront the despair brought on by hardship. This trust
is, in reality, faith in the Creator. From the narrow
point of view of the concept of revelation, however, it
cannot be interpreted as such. And when, on the everyday level, man weathers the storm without having had
knowledge of Jesus in his soul, from the narrow perspective of the concept of revelation this does not appear
as anything particularly positive. Rather, from this
point of view such success becomes disquieting. "Christian" faith seems to be threatened by such positive processes.

       The result is that true faith in its fulness is
actually destroyed. Those elements of Creation faith
which operate during times of despair and destruction in
our everyday situation, whether in the life of a Christian
or non-Christian, are not treated as faith, but are depre-
ciated as "shallow optimism" or the like. Actually, however, these elements of faith and this elementary courage
to face life must be life construed as a form of life
that is supported by the Second and Third Articles.

       To abolish this undue theorization and to return the
Christian faith to those human situations where it belongs
is perhaps the most important task for contemporary theology. In our present cultural situation this task can only
be performed in one way. Human life as such must be analyzed, and in the analysis we must strive to show that
life building factors are given to us (rather than pro-
duced by us) and that destructive factors inevitably in-
trude where life is lived. No morality has the power to
create life or to abolish destruction.

       This phenomenological analysis of human life as such

is what K. E. Løgstrup has performed in his epoch-making
books, most clearly in *The Ethical Demand* (1956).[57]   The
point of his analysis is that it is possible to discover
God and the Devil in life *without* having to use the terms
"God" or "Devil" at all.

Løgstrup began writing in 1947, but the full consequence of his approach was still obscure to me.
It was therefore not possible at that time for me to
make use of his analysis in order philosophically to criticize Bultmann, Nygren, and Barth. That was a task Løgstrup himself later carried out. I came to Basel instead
with historical investigations in my luggage. Moreover,
as a historian I had real cause for protest, since the
Christological method within the reigning theology laid
claim on Luther for present-day use. Accordingly, in my
criticism of European theology after 1920 I focused attention on theological method.

The result was that my book *Theology in Conflict*
became bound to certain concepts which were especially
important for the Reformation in the sixteenth century,
namely the Law in its relation to the Gospel or kerygma.[58]
Furthermore, where Irenaeus is occasionally given attention, it is the problem of "Law and Gospel" that dominates
the exposition (*Theology in Conflict,* pp. 93-100) in spite
of the fact that this problem, typical of the Reformation,
occupies a fairly peripheral place in the theology of the
Church Fathers and their polemic against the Gnostics. Of
course, a thorough analysis of the relation between Law
and Gospel is important. [In Løgstrup's philosophical
analyses this relation between "the universal" (the Law)
and "the specific" (the Gospel) also plays quite a central
role.] But the two concepts, Law on the one hand and Gospel on the other, must be given their place in the larger

context in which they belong, something I did not do in
Theology in Conflict.

The source of the Law is not the preaching of the
church but God's work in Creation. The Law exists before the Gospel. Moreover, it always preserves life;
it is always, even in depraved form, more beneficial to
life than chaos is. The Law is never free from destructive elements. Therefore within particular communities,
cultures, and eras, new laws are always being made and
old laws are being altered or abolished. This unceasing
change which goes on in all states may be interpreted
theologically: both the new Creation of God and the destruction of the Devil are going on continually on earth.[59]

Only against this background does the uniqueness of
the kerygma concerning the death and resurrection of Christ
as a "justification without deeds" that is alien to the
Law in all its forms become plain. For if the world that
surrounds us is emptied of "Creation and Law," then the
inevitable result will be profound secularization of the
church. In this situation the Law, which is for the regulation of the world, must have come from the church. The
church then becomes a legislative body and Jesus the great
legislator. The totally new and creative work of the Gospel ceases to be the center of the concept of the church.
Instead, by necessity it becomes a political institution
which supplies programs for solving the many changing
problems of earthly society. For a time this may have a
vitalizing effect on a church which has often fled from
the world, but in the long run secularization has the opposite effect: it generates reactionary attempts to escape into narrow, fundamentalistic groups.

Even today we witness the emergence of such reactionary groups. The criticism usually leveled at them

is all too often that they "forget the political consequences of the Gospel," as the phrase goes. When we
want to criticize someone, however, we should first point
out where he is actually right.

   And indeed, it can be said that there really is in
the New Testament descriptions of the content of the Gospel a surprising indifference to the question of the human consequences of the Gospel in the earthly realm. The
indifference on this point stems from the enormous inner
assurance and joy with which the first Christian congregation was prepared to meet death. All through the New
Testament it is obvious that these early Christians felt
an electric shock which emanated from the discovery of
the empty tomb on Easter morning. The Gospel loses this
joy and "electricity" if it is turned into a Law for politics.

   The God who raises Jesus from the dead surely desires only what is good for the body. The Bible bears
witness to this in the Old Testament with all its laws
and in the story of the Creation with all living things
around about man. God as Creator is active in the whole
world, and from his created works emanates the Law. In
the resurrection on the third day the Creator performs a
new deed, only performed in a single person, Jesus Christ,
but a deed nonetheless for whose continuation the church
waits because it believes in the word of the Gospel.
Therefore the church looks forward in hope. No scornful
words claiming that the Christian faith is, with this focus on death and resurrection, "the opiate of the masses"
should be allowed to hinder theology today from clinging
to this radical eschatological hope contained in the Gospel.

   In response to escapist religious groups, one must

indeed point out that God is the God of the whole world
and that here on earth he is involved in the human per-
formance of external and bodily acts, even in those with
short effect.[60] In establishing the earthly goals toward
which these acts are directed, the members of the Christian community live under the Law together with the rest
of mankind. The First Article of faith understood in
these terms can never become a surrogate for the Gospel.
On the contrary, the clearer the contours of Creation and
Law stand out, the clearer becomes the framework in which
the preaching of the Gospel and the expectation of the
Christian church for another kingdom is found.

        "Creation and Law," "Gospel and Church"—these four
terms in precisely this order should constitute the foundation of the dogmatic construction to succeed the theology
of the 1920s. Only with a construction of this type can
we get behind the Enlightenment back to a biblical theology. That is what it means to go backwards in order to
move forward. And it is a movement forward because the
biblical message, when we at last get hold of it, is meant
to be preached.

An Historian Being Converted

        To assert in a theological and academic context
in Sweden that the biblical word "is meant to be preached"
is scandalous. It was scandalous as early as 1949 when I
formulated this assertion in *The Living Word*. I have since
then continuously stated this thesis without it becoming
less scandalous.

        That means that during my whole stint as full pro-
fessor at the University of Lund I stood outside what is
considered respectable in Swedish theology. That fact has
meant that in Sweden I have not been able to alter the

established view of what scientific theology is since
Anders Nygren's earliest books (1921-3). The same has
been true in Finland, where the universities also pro-
claim Nygren's view. Nygren's theories about the scientific character of theology have not been accepted beyond these two countries. It is unfortunate that Swedish
theology is becoming more and more isolated.

Thanks to my approach in *The Living Word* (1949),
however, I have been in dialogue with many other theologians in Europe, in spite of my criticism of Barth and
Bultmann and of the schools of thought of which they are
the founders. What connects me with them is the kerygmatic approach.

The surprising thing about Nygren is his combination
of a strictly scientific attitude and a directly reactionary ecclesiastical attitude. For example, Nygren and the
former Bishop of Gothenburg, Bo Giertz, represent the intellectual foundation of opposition against the ordination of women. To this day in these circles reference is
made to Nygren's reservations about the Church Synod of
1958, when the law concerning the ordination of women
was passed. Nygren assumed a markedly conservative attitude during his time as Bishop in Lund on several other
questions too.

But this strange combination of a conservative,
status quo view of the church and a strict view of science
as free from evaluations is not as surprising as it may at
first seem. The link between them is the historical ideal
of theology: that is, the idea that strictly scientific
theology involves the correct description, within the university context, of something that has to do with the
history of the church, which is understood as fixed and given.

The thesis that the biblical text as it exists in

its historical connections is "meant to be preached" means
that this old text came into being only in order to be delivered to men other than the writers, and that the text
can be understood only when it is thus delivered to new
people. For Swedish theology, however, this is tanta-
mount to "mixing history with the present." It destroys
the possibility of "scientific" work. The church may do
this, but not theologians in the university milieu. Further, such a thesis also means that "assertions and evaluations are mixed up." An "ought" is brought into a purely descriptive, historical investigation. The preacher
in the pulpit may do this, but not the scholar at the university.

Such statements directed against the Continental
kerygmatic approach were uttered as early as 1949, when
my book *The Living Word* was published. They are still asserted today by Swedish university theologians, at Uppsala
as well as Lund.

Why weren't Nygren and I immediately engaged in open
conflict when *The Living Word,* a publicly known and vigorously debated book, was first published? I am not certain.
Only after *Theology in Conflict* was published in 1954, however, did the conflict break out. (Our debate was carried
on in several issues of "*Svensk teologisk kvartalskrift,*"
1956.) I am still a bit surprised that the conflict was
delayed as long as it was.

In *The Living Word* I stated plainly and clearly that
I was critical of the historicizing method of Swedish theology. Around that time I also announced a book, which was
to be devoted entirely to the question of methodology in
theology, in which I intended critically to examine Nygren,
Bring, Barth, and Bultmann.[61] There should have been no
occasion for surprise when this promised book was

published in 1954.

We can begin, at this juncture, a discussion of the kerygmatic approach by pointing out that the bridge between "going backwards" to the Bible in order to "go ahead" to preaching is a central point in the Gospel: the repetition of the spoken word. In New Testament times it was never thought to be enough to present the Gospel once to each individual. If that had been the case, the New Testament letters would never have been written. But written they were. The word was also proclaimed in early Christian worship services; texts from the scriptures served as the foundation for sermons or oral speech.

The oral character of primitive Christianity should not surprise us, for Jesus and the first disciples lived in a culture dominated by scribes and overwhelmed with scrolls. There is not a single passage in the New Testament in which Jesus writes anything, except the very significant moment when he bends down and writes on the ground. Note that even at this point nothing is said about what it was that he wrote (John 8:6). There was, of course, no contempt for the written and determinate word; there is no tendency toward "mysticism" in the nonscribal character of primitive Christianity. Yet it is quite plain that formulas in which "the Gospel" is concentrated are passed down by tradition (1 Cor. 15:1-5) and that this was done orally. All four Gospels conclude by saying that Jesus sent persons out into the world with *words* to *speak*.

These concluding Gospel stories are stories about the resurrected Jesus. If, as historians, we adopt a hypercritical attitude and assert that there is in these last stories not a single element which actually happened, but only reconstructions after the fact that were

made because of the needs of the church, then the oral
character becomes even more astounding. For we know that
the church in A.D. 70 began to construct scriptures from
existing documents—that is, from written rather than
oral tradition. Now, if the church after the fact reconstructed the events mentioned last in the four Gospels—
the ascension of Jesus and the commissioning of the
apostles—then the church could just as well have constructed a command from Jesus to commit the events to
writing, commands such as exist, for example, in Revelation (Rev. 1:11 and several other places).

But no one puts the word "write" into the mouth of
Jesus as a commission given by him at the end of the Gospel story. There is rather a complete dominance of the
spoken word. In addition it should be noted that the
Acts of the Apostles is concerned precisely with travel-
ling and *speaking* apostles. To this must be added the
fact that when as a fanatic persecutor of the Christians
Paul traveled to Damascus, he did so with the aim of ex-
terminating a group of Christians already there who had
not, as of that time, yet acquired any New Testament
scripture (Acts 9:2). Finally, it is worth noting that
there was already a Christian community in Rome without
any New Testament scripture before Paul ever journeyed
there, and that, despite the fact that Rome had already
received his letter.

The oral tradition of primitive Christianity is a
historical miracle and should be used as the foundation
for the definition of "the Gospel." This can be expressed
in a specific thesis: the Gospel in its original purity
was an oral message that was proclaimed in town after town;
it was *not* a text.

But this dimension is in no way the most surprising

indication of the fundamental dependence of Christianity
on the spoken word. If from among the confessions of
church history we were to select the one that is most
text-bound, we would select Lutheranism. But we would
find that in fact the starting point even there consisted
of a radically oral word often fixed in the form of a
program by Luther himself. According to Luther the
deeper the meaning behind the written word was to inspire
oral speech. "It is not according to the New Testament
to write books" he says. "There should," he continues,
"be preachers without books in all places.... That it was
necessary to write books is already a great diminishing
of the Spirit." This view of Luther's concerning the
emergence of the four Gospels is gravely offensive to
the confessional Lutheran. But, as usual, Luther hit the
mark with this thesis about historical conditions in the
beginning of primitive Christianity.[62]

   If the word is intended to be spoken, naturally it
becomes characterized by repetitiveness. If an external
event has taken place (and the Gospel tells us of external
events), then it ought to be enough to give information
about this event once, preferably in writing; if necessary,
orally. The one to whom this word is delivered is informed about certain facts. But the Gospel is not communicated in this way. Rather, the Gospel is repeated, and
varied, for its words are more than informative. In fact,
the situation to which these words of the Gospel are addressed is a fallen one in which there are forces at work
that are actively opposed to the Gospel. Therefore the
word of the Gospel as it reaches the ears of the listener
may be compared to food and drink in our mouths. For, to
stick with "bodily" terminology, whoever receives the
word eats the word, and he does this because of hunger,

that is to say, because of a condition that makes him soon have to eat again. In the same way, because of our fallen condition, the Gospel is active in the listener and the event needs to be *repeated* again.

This fact points out a parallel between the Gospel on the one hand and Baptism and Holy Communion on the other. All of these are events that picture something which is reenacted *in* the listener, *in* the person baptized, and *in* the communicant member. However, they do this in different ways. At this point we must first treat somewhat more extensively the inner connection between the Gospel and the sermon.

The oral speaking involved in the sermon contains no special external bodily actions as Baptism and Holy Communion do. But since the sermon is a narrative built on epic elements, as the four Gospels are, it portrays things in its peculiar way. For many centuries, this epic character underlay the church's use of traditional ' pericopes of the Gospel as the only lessons for the mass. The same texts were expounded year after year. The basis for this arrangement was the belief that the year as such tells a story (or is an "ecclesiastical year," as we now express it). Christmas, Easter, and Pentecost are the basic building-blocks of a narrative year.

Accordingly, it was also natural that the main text of each day should have been a narrative, not an exposition of doctrine. Thus the whole idea of having the Gospel stories present at the center of the service is in principle one of retelling these same events. The system is then a yearly repetition of the narrative of the Gospel, one which is reinforced by the permanent epic poetry of Baptism and Holy Communion, that is, the immersion in water, the emergence, the breaking of the bread, and so on.

In the course of time paintings on the walls of the church building were added which usually represented series of epic events taken scene by scene from the Gospels. Everywhere there was the picture of Jesus, the only real man who remained eternally young. Church paintings are only one example, however, of the tremendous impact this one man, with his brief life, had on European art. Even more remarkable, though, is Jesus' total permeation of history. The events of his life have had an objective impact on the way in which every European population looks at each year.[63] "It was just before Easter," or "it was about Christmas of that year" is what everyone says when trying to remember and to identify something. Moreover, people even speak this Gospel-narrative language when they look forward and plan. The events of the life of Jesus have determined the western calendar.

Gospel texts were used on ordinary Sundays as well as at the great festivals. Since between Jesus' birth (Christmas) and resurrection (Easter) lies his active life, which is recalled in Gospels that relate these acts or events of which he is in some way the center, the Sundays between Pentecost and Christmas continued with extracts from the Gospels. These texts retained their epic form and were as free from didactic material as they were on the great festival days.

The sermon has been based on this epic material through the ages. The basically oral character of the Gospels means that the written and recited texts are intended to be spoken and heard by the people gathered at the worship service.

Today we would be able to acquire a clear conception of what this meant in times past only if we were illiterate.

Certainly the greater share of those who have, during the
course of the world's history, told or listened to stories have been illiterate. Their ability to tell and lis-
ten remained, nevertheless, unimpaired. On the contrary,
without a doubt they were more skillful than we in both
the art of narration and of listening. Communication
among people of times past took place on a more basic
level and had longer-lasting effects than does our communication, which is often superficial.

The following three points are of special importance with regard to the narration of the epic events of
the Gospels. First, the text or sermon paints a picture
of a person on a road from birth to death. These texts
tell us of Jesus and fix a picture of him in the soul of
the listener. Since the listener himself walks the same
road, that is, the road from birth to death, there is
awakened in him an inclination to imitate the picture, to
enter into a "following" of him who is the focus of the
Gospels. This elementary summons to follow what is pic-
tured is rooted in the texts and in no way involves a
moralistic misunderstanding of the Gospel.

Second, the text and the sermon picture a whole
string of figures that surround Jesus, the main figure.
These are the blind, the lame, the publicans, and the
adulterers. Seldom do we find Jesus by himself. Precisely because of this the Gospel can become a call to its
hearers. If the texts were didactic, it would be perfectly suitable for the teacher to be by himself. But the
text is the story of someone who *does* something. Therefore he is surrounded by hundreds of people who all represent the person for whom Jesus does this something. That
is, every person portrayed is an instance of "Adamic mankind." And the thing to note about each of them is that

in every case there is something lacking. Even the
twelve apostles misunderstand the Gospel, for they have
not yet reached the goal, which Jesus embodies, but are
on their way, following the picture formed by his life.
The illiterate listener of all times can identify himself with these persons.

Third, the fellowship between the main figure,
Jesus, and those who surround him is not broken. The
very character of the Gospel consists of this unbroken-
ness and it is this that is the *"eu"* (the good) of the
Greek *euangelion* (Good News). The reason for the prefix
eu (good) in the message of these texts has to do with
the man to whom the Gospel is directed. That is, the
news of the Gospel is "good" exactly for the figures for
whom the main figure does something and who thus receive
the healing and forgiveness which he bestows. Hence,
every listener himself becomes a receiver. And herein
lies the aim of the act of preaching: the transferral of
the benefits of Jesus' activity to new recipients. This
is the work of the Spirit in the church. Because of the
objective content of the texts the hearer of the word is
not hindered from receiving on account of his faults,
mistakes and weaknesses. Even if the hearer is a criminal just about to be executed, he can receive the whole
kingdom of heaven from the text. He is then the criminal
next to Jesus on the cross at Golgotha.[64]

The epic character of a text of this kind has a far
stronger effect on the hearers of the word than does the
clarity and sharpness of an abstract doctrine. To say
"God justifies man without regard to his merit" is on the
factual level the same thing as telling the story of the
prodigal son or the story of the malefactor on the cross.
In a theological debate the abstract thesis is most suit-

able. But the person who listens to an abstract doctrine explained in a sermon sees no human picture.

The church avoided placing abstract theses in the
center of the service when it constructed a narrative
year that encircled the lives of all listeners. The
Gospel was instead a story told at every morning service
the year around. And it is a great mistake to believe
that such an arrangement is suitable only for illiterates.
A highly sophisticated modern intellectual may only discover this for himself when, for instance, he sees Jesus'
story performed on the stage of a theatre. It is then
that he meets it in its original form. Suddenly the epic
character of the story is regained and *the human picture*
functions again. Today the construction of services in
the official churches generally obscures the element of
story, partly because of purely didactic and abstract sermons and partly because of attempts to be modern and up-
to-date, which involve abandoning the text and thereby its
naive epic character. The renaissance of the picture of
Jesus in secular literature and art is, at this point, of
benefit to the church for it is what is concrete that
"preaches."

Historically the collecting of the texts that we
now call "the Bible" occurred because of the need in the
Christian worship services for words that were intended
to be repeated and expounded to new groups of people. If
we do away with this use of the Bible—that is, no longer
let the Bible function in the present through preaching—
we lose what makes the Bible distinctive. Unfortunately
this dimension of the Bible has been ignored by a historicizing theology which is trying to convince itself of its
strictly scientific character.

Nowhere in the Hebrew or Greek texts are the terms

"Bible," "Old Testament," and "New Testament" used. A
linguist, an unbiased philologist, who goes back to the
pure "texts" will never find an "Old" or "New Testament."
These terms have been appended to the texts by the Christian church; they were not originally found in them. In
the church service, and only in the service, were these
labels attached.[65] If we imagine that the supposedly exact disciplines of "New Testament" and "Old Testament"
exegesis can place the Bible in a museum as an object devoid of preaching elements, in order that it may be analyzed in a value-free and objective manner, we are terri-
bly mistaken. On the contrary, the element of evaluation
—or, if you will, of preaching—is even built into the
names of the scientific disciplines at the universities.

The fact of the conflict with Anders Nygren and his
"motif research," which was, from the standpoint of my
importation of the Continental kerygmatic approach, inevitable, should not have led interested onlookers to believe that *The Living Word* of 1949 represented an isolated
and solitary wing in the house of Swedish theology. In
fact, no Swedish theologian today, either in Uppsala or
in Lund, works expressly with Nygren's scientific method.
Instead, what has succeeded motif research is very strongly dependent upon Anglo-American analytical philosophy
(Axel Gyllenkrok, Hampus Lyttkens, Ragnar Holte, Anders
Jeffner, Jarl Hemberg). This means that Swedish theology
today diverges somewhat from Nygren's program of treating
Christianity as a historical fact: no one speaks any
longer of his three basic motifs, *Agape, Eros,* and *Nomos.*
But with respect to the question of what is constitutive
for *science*, every contemporary Swedish systematician
still follows Nygren's footsteps.

Contemporary Swedish theologians totally reject the

Continental kerygmatic approach.[66] In this Sweden dif-
fers remarkably from Denmark and Norway, where the theological faculties and work carried on there received strong
impulses from the European continent, especially West Germany and Switzerland. I am thinking especially of Regin
Prenter, K. E. Løgstrup, Theodor Jørgensen and Ole Jensen
in Denmark; and of Johan B. Hygen and Inge Lønning in
Norway. At this point nothing indicates that the cooperation of Danish and Norwegian theologians with the
leading systematicians and exegetes of the European continent will diminish in extent or intensity. In fact,
the connections southward are increasing. At the same
time the communication lines of *Swedish* systematic theologians are fixed in a single westward direction towards
the English-speaking countries.

     Another factor which contributes to Sweden's theo-
logical isolation is the sharp barrier that New Testament
exegetes have erected against every attempt to place any
form of "kerygma," in the manner of Rudolf Bultmann, at
the center of the New Testament. The "Form Critical
School," of which Bultmann is a founder, is vehemently rejected by Swedish New Testament exegetes (Harald Riesenfeld and Birger Garhardsson), at the same time that demythologization is rejected, or rather destroyed by silence, in Swedish systematic theology.

     Though it is true that, early on, exegetes at Uppsala
and Lund established relations with German exegetes, they
did not establish them with the representatives of the
Form Critical method. Rather, they made contact with
that minority of German scholars who worked with Rabbinic
Judaism. Thus, for them, the conception of an oral tradition emanating from Jesus himself that was carried on in
a Rabbinic manner by the apostles took the place of the

idea of the primitive Christian kerygma and its present
proclamation, the idea to which Bultmann and the Form
Critics had assigned the central role.[67] The combination of a Swedish systematic theology influenced by analytical philosophy (and therefore negative about any
kind of kerygmatic approach) and a Swedish exegetical
theology influenced by the Rabbinic idea of "tradition,"
created a scientific climate in Sweden that made my book
The Living Word look completely bizarre, which is how it
is still perceived to this very day.

The situation on the European continent is different. In German *Die Predigt* has gone through three editions, of which one is a completely new reprint in East
Germany. Since the whole manner of argumentation is connected to Barth's and Bultmann's "theology of the Word,"
the exposition fits into the Continental debate. Moreover
the chronological somersault to which English-American
readers were subjected (*Theology in Conflict* appeared
first in English in 1958, while *The Living Word* was delayed until 1960) never occurred in the German-speaking
countries. *Die Predigt* was published in its first edition
in 1955, *Die Methodenfrage* in 1957—the same order as in
Sweden. The whole procedure of *first* analyzing what
preaching means and only *later* raising the question of
theological method was thereby made fully intelligible
in the German-speaking area of Europe.

Furthermore, the subject matter of *The Living Word*
is biblical: a great many Bible texts, both Old and New,
are given prominent consideration. These texts are not
pressed into a Lutheran pattern; on the contrary, in an
important section on Law and its relations to the body
Martin Luther is made the object of a direct and central
criticism based on biblical texts. In the English trans-

lation this section is placed under a special heading entitled "Excursus: Emphasis on the Outward in the New
Testament and in Luther's Thought."[68] When my book on
theological method came along, my perspective narrowed,
since I then concentrated on Barth's, Bultmann's and Nygren's claim to have revived the Reformation against
Liberalism in their theological work. Because of this,
Luther and the opposition between Law and Gospel are
given a far more prominent place in *Theology in Conflict*
than in *The Living Word*.

But if the kerygmatic approach links me to Continental theology, it is at the same time obvious that on
the question of theological content I markedly dissociate
myself from the interpretation of Barth and Bultmann. My
divergence from their pattern lies primarily in my view
of the hearers of the word and their situation when the
word reaches them. I usually describe these hearers and
their situation with the formula "Creation and Law." But
as the cry of a herald always has its meaning partially
determined by the specific situation of the listeners,
that is, by the situation of distress into which the cry
of the herald is voiced, how "Creation and Law" are conceived will secondarily also affect one's conception of
"Gospel and Church." Anthropological conditions affect
one's hermeneutics.[69] This inner connection between the
interpretation of "texts" and the interpretation of "man"
is articulated in several passages in *The Living Word*.

The reader of *The Living Word* could find, as early
as 1949, a marked divergence from Barth and Bultmann on
two points. First, against Barth I argue that the words
of Christ to man are *not* a communication of knowledge
about a God who is unknown outside of the Gospel. Second, I argue against Bultmann that the body and matter

are at every moment affected by and included in the activity of God, both under the Law and in liberation
from the Law. These two points are closely connected.
Both Law *and* Gospel are actions of the Creator by which
he advances the work that he began in Creation and fin-
ishes in the resurrection of the dead. That is, both
Law and Gospel involve, above all, acts in God's struggle against a destruction that affects the body, a struggle through which the body is made free.

But the important thing about *The Living Word* is
not its particular divergence from Continental theology, but
its overreaching connection with it; important, too, is
my corresponding divergence from Swedish theology in
nearly all areas, including dogmatics, ethics, philosophy
of religion, exegesis and practical theology.

Two factors have contributed to the isolation of
these areas of theological inquiry in Sweden from the
work being done on the Continent.

On the one hand, after the end of World War II a
a militant, antichristian attitude (Ingemar Hedenius) [70]
which stemmed from the analytical philosophy at the Swedish universities, especially Uppsala, arose and led to
attempts to remove the theological faculties from the
universities. The attackers were concerned only to a
small degree with dogmatic questions. On the other hand
the traditional subject of "Christian theology" was altered within the Swedish educational system so as to include general knowledge of world religions and different
views of life. The theological faculties willingly accepted the role of providing "religion" teachers with an
education of the kind that the school, but naturally not
the church, demanded.

The kerygmatic approach, which presupposes that

biblical texts are preached in the present situation, necessarily appears unusuable in such a situation. Since the needs of the schools now govern Swedish theology, the education of the clergy is secondarily fitted into university education, which in principle no longer takes the church into consideration. Modern Swedish theology has clearly and unmistakeably betrayed the Swedish church.

The result is that a large group within the present Swedish clergy cling to the theology of times past—and especially to such older authorities as supplied arguments against the ordination of women in the early '50s (Anders Nygren, Anton Friedrichsen, Hugh Odesberg, Harald Riesenfeld). The clergy and the institutional church, rather than the preaching of the word of the Gospel, stubbornly maintain their place at the center of attention in the Swedish church today.

Before much longer the Swedish church will loosen its ties to the state. But when the Swedish school system is finally emancipated from the church and Christianity, the only reasonable alternative for the future will be a *stronger* rather than a weaker articulation of the Christian message, a task which will belong, then, only to the church. Yet the two theological faculties of Sweden have chosen a different way: they organize their scientific work according to the needs of the schools. Therefore the kerygmatic approach, which is so typical of the European continent, is an impossibility in Sweden. Probably many upheavals will shake the Swedish church before it becomes possible to make room for a healthy theology conscious of its specific task.

Until then, I am convinced, the essential theological tasks will remain untreated within the Swedish faculties at Uppsala and Lund, awaiting the day when it is

accepted that theology must begin with the biblical text
and that the biblical text, on its part, becomes meaningful only as a text *preached* in the present.

IV. CREATION, LAW, GOSPEL, CHURCH

Creation and Work

According to Friedrich Gogarten, Christian belief in Creation is the origin of freedom in relation to
the world. In pre-Christian religions it was thought that
the world was permeated with secret powers. Everywhere
a divinity was hidden: in the river, in the mountain, in
the thunder, in the shrub and tree. One had to be care-
ful to offer sacrifices and worship. From precisely this
veneration of what surrounds man on earth the Christian
faith brings liberation. There is only one God, the Creator. In the world that he has created there is nothing
divine. The world is *nur Welt*—only world—as Gogarten
says.[72]

The very fact that the world is created should
then, according to Gogarten, give man freedom and sovereignty vis-á-vis what he confronts. It is typical of
Gogarten that this freedom, moreover, is a freedom *in the
world*. He ties this talk of freedom to an exegesis of Gal.
4:1-7, which is expounded in such a way that the Christian's attitude of freedom with respect to the earth
actually becomes the core of the good "inheritance" that
man is given through belief in God.[73] With a certain
triumphant tone, Gogarten asserts that modern secularization is a gift which Christianity has given to western
civilization.

When these theses were first presented by Gogarten
and other theologians in the middle of the twentieth

century, secularization and the "dominion" over nature
that follows from it were in an unproblematic way conceived of as something good. At that time theologians
desired to show that this good came from Christianity.
Soon afterwards, however, by the end of the 1960s, insight into the dark side of "dominion," namely the pollution of the environment, began to deepen. (Some time
back a few persons wished to warn us, but they were then
disdainfully called "Doomsday prophets.") Now, when
knowledge about the devastating effects of our western
civilization on surrounding nature is almost daily expressed in every newspaper, the tone of the theologians
regarding the biblical idea of "dominion" is somewhat
less triumphant. Their increasing timidity is justified.

One might say that Gogarten is both right and wrong
in his thesis about the worth of secularization. The following might be said about this process: when we observe
African and Asiatic cultures, it strikes us that to them
nature is not bereft of its religious dimension. The
holy cows of India are by no means the only example. Nature is believed to be fraught with power over man: the
springs, the rain, the thunder, the vegetation represent
a play of forces to which man is subject. In contrast,
the West (Europe and America) has more or less robbed nature of its mysterious role, so that what is all around
us is viewed as something that we have at our disposal.
As Gogarten points out, the most important factor in the
European development has been belief in Creation. In this
tradition the sentence "God is the Creator of the world"
divests the earth of all divinity. The world becomes *nur
Welt*—only world. But though we must make this distinction between the Creator and his creation, we must not do
so in such a way as to cast off nature's religious dimension

More than the thesis that "God is the Creator of
the earth" is required, of course, in order that this process of desacralization can be seen as having been begun.
A detail like the absence of images (Israel, for example,
forbade the making of images) is essential, for no object
or process on earth depicts the true God. All elements
and processes of nature lie powerlessly spread out over
the surface of the earth, for all are under him. No man
has ever seen God. He is only heard "in the Word" which
he sends through the mouths of his prophets. With a mix-
ture of scorn and anger Deutero-Isaiah (Isaiah 40:18-31)
describes the man who makes idols and bows down to them.
The thesis that God is Creator, in its radical biblical
form, implies this conscious rejection of every attempt
at making God visible. No matter what the eye of man
falls upon when he looks around himself, he remains certain that nothing in this world is worthy of worship and
that nothing stands above him. On the contrary, all of
nature lies beneath him. He is the "rule" and has dominion over all, as commanded in the second part of the
story of Creation: when all was created mankind was
called to "rule" the whole earth; man and woman together
are given this task by God (Gen. 1:26-28).

It is clarifying, however, to specify at this point
exactly which element of Creation faith plays the decisive
role in modern "theologies of secularity." The accent
throughout falls on the concept *nur Welt,* that is, on the
idea of desacralization. A peculiar apologetical bifurca-
tion marks this theology. On the one hand there is the
wish to appropriate the modern technical civilization
characteristic of the West and to find its origin in
biblical Creation faith. On the other hand, there is the
emphasis that reason—and not, for example, the word of

the Bible—is decisive in the worldly community. It is
to mankind, *all* of mankind, independent of religious
faith, that the power to rule over nature has been given.

Undoubtedly the Creation story carries this meaning.
That is, it is a fact that man governs created things and
animals, just as it is a fact that for our sustenance we
are dependent on sun and rain. The Creation story aims
at describing a general human situation that is simply
there, independent of whether there is a church on earth
or not. The same holds true for Luther's doctrine of
the earthly realm, the realm where "reason" (and not the
word of the Bible) governs the measures that are taken.

Within the modern theology, that, with "secularization" as its banner, today exploits the biblical Creation story and the theses that the Reformers directed
against the medieval system, the whole accent falls on
freedom from ecclesiastical guardianship and authority.

There is, however, yet another side of Creation
faith that at present plays a very subordinate role. We
do not catch sight of this aspect if we compare Christianity to the primitive religions that see gods in springs,
thunderstorms and other phenomena of nature. Instead, it
is to the philosophical roots of western thought that we
must turn.

In Greek philosophy from Plato onward the body and
the rest of the phenomenal world are emptied of spiritual
importance, for they are "lower." "Desacralization" had
already taken place, partly with the help of terms that
appear to show a certain resemblance to the vocabulary of
the Old Testament story of Creation. Reason is to govern
the body and the instincts, subjugating these lower phenomena. But actually the difference between the Greek and
Old Testament views is enormous. Let us quickly determine

one or two of these important differences between the
Israelite-Jewish view of Greek philosophy.

According to Israel the whole world is created. It
is positively instituted by God as well as ordered. It
is not formless matter or raw material to which man must
give form, rather, according to the faith of Israel, man
administers a world ordered beforehand. Israel therefore had a respect and a reverence for the body that the
Greek philosopher did not have. For example, a Rabbi
was to have a handicraft as an occupation, while the wise
men of Greece despised menial work.

Moreover, "he who really is" (Jahve), according to
the belief of Israel, governed the peoples and acted in
the political and military clamor in which Assyria and
Egypt crossed swords over the little Israel. On the other hand, to the philosopher "what really is" is only ac-
cessible by means of abstraction from "the changeable," as
he calls it.

The deliverance from Egypt and the rescue from
Babylon were political events to which the prophets continually returned to find insight about the will of God
for this earthly sphere. But no philosopher thought that
it would be possible to gain any ethical knowledge from
similar events in Greek history, such as the battle of
Marathon and the battle of Salamis.

It would be possible to continue this comparison
point by point. At every juncture, however, one would
find the same thing, namely an aversion to "the lower" on
the part of the Greek philosophers, and reverence and respect for "the body" created by God among the Israelites.[74]

A real collision between these two views did not take
place until the period of the early church in which contempt for the body had increased dramatically in the dif-

ferent Gnostic movements, with the consequence that the
Old Testament was repudiated. Gnosticism was the most
serious enemy of the young martyr church, and it was in
response to this deadly threat that the early church constructed its Trinitarian Creed, in which, as one could
expect, the sentence about the Creator comes first.

The tone of this affirmation of the Creator was,
however, different from that which is characteristic of
"the theology of secularity" today. Since the Gnostic
despised the body, and the church said: "the body is
good, so good that God wills its existence and its salvation." The savior himself lived in an earthly body that
was crucified and laid in a tomb, one which was not able
to contain him. The Gospel is a *yes* to the body. And
in these anti-Gnostic early church assertions we encounter
the spirit of Martin Luther, for his opposition to the
Middle Ages cannot be enclosed *solely* in his doctrine of
freedom in relation to the worldly realm and the church.
This latter accent in Luther was due in large part to the
exigencies of the sixteenth century milieu. It is there,
however, and it is this accent which is excessively used
in modern theology's rejoicing about secularization. But
the early church accent on the goodness of the body allows
God rather than the Church to work in the external world
and constantly create anew.

It is really only a question of two *accents.* There
is no real conflict between the two points of which we
are now speaking. Each point may be emphasized at different times, as, for instance, they are in Luther. His
emphasis simply shifts a bit when the polemical point moves
from one enemy to another. When he speaks of the independence of the civil community in the face of church supremacy—with regard to the medieval confusion of princely

with church power, then his accent falls on the freedom and independence of the worldly realm from the church and her message. Automatically then, man as man has authority vis-á-vis the church in all that does not concern "salvation"; that is to say, in all that does not concern the proclamation of the Gospel. It is on this point that today's "secular theology" has focused.

But in the persecuted early church there was no connection between princes and bishops. Hence, in the writing of that time there is no polemical point with this accent. Rather, faith in the Creator was threatened by the Gnostics, who continually separated the body from relationship to God and from salvation. They asserted that the "demiurge," and not God, created the world, that Christ came in a shadow body, since the womb would have been too unclean for him, and that the body was not to be resurrected and saved on the last day. None of these Gnostics, however, cooperated with the heathen emperor of Rome or any other sovereign. They were only the "intellectuals" of that time. And against them the church built its Creed in Three Articles, each expressing itself in opposition to every Gnostic heresy: (1) "Maker of heaven and *earth*"; (2) "*Born* of the Virgin Mary...*suffered...crucified, dead* and *buried*"; (3) "I believe in the resurrection of the *body*" (*resurrectio carnis*). Here the accent was not placed on the freedom of "the body" or "the earth" from church control. It falls on God's will and desire to be near the body. He loves the body and wills its life from beginning to end. God wills our work on earth.

If we want to meet Luther in these anti-Gnostic, early church affirmations then we must not read his attacks on the papacy. Instead, we must study his polemics against monastic life, the monastic vows, and celibacy.

Intercourse between man and woman is an act that is
willed by God and one through which he *now* creates.   It
is not the case that God was once Creator and is now
something else.   According to Luther, he is Creator *today*.   And the act of Creation in intercourse leads directly to the nourishment and care of the child.   All
acts of work like these which cause nutrition to reach
the hungering and clothing to be given to those who are
cold and violence to be prevented from affecting the de-
fenseless——all of these earthly tasks are in the service
of the Creator, who chooses life over death.   Luther's
explanation of the First Article gives this fundamental
view in a simple and childlike form.

     This side of faith in God as the Creator of the
earth plays a minor role in modern "secular theology."
It is almost as if, in this theology, there is a fear
that God might come too close to the earth and the body.
The regulating and controlling rule of the church threatens to appear again!   This reservation is, I suspect, an
indication of how persistently the idea remains that if
God works among us in the present, then he must be doing
so through *the church*.   It is strange that the relatively
recent idea that mankind's contact with God comes through
the church has been able to bind the imaginations of so
many people.

     This concentration on the church is actually one of
the consequences of an unexpected vacuum in the field of
anthropology that has been brought about by the two leading twentieth century philosophies, existentialism and
analytical philosophy.   No objective reasons can be given,
according to these philosophies, for ethical statements.
They rest rather on a subjective judgment or, as it is
called on the Continent, on an *Entscheidung*, or decision.

Classical theology, however, until the twentieth century, acknowledged the existence of protective mechanisms for the defense of physical life that are built right into human life—the same kind of mechanisms as exist in the animal world. It also acknowledged that these mechanisms express themselves in laws that the individual cannot evade. Especially as regards the erotic relation between man and woman such natural laws were thought to be manifest apart from the church's having to introduce them into human life. It was thought that they existed within the creation itself as laws that naturally are not nullified when some people break them.

Modern philosophy's rejection of these earlier ideas of "a natural good" and modern theology's emphasis on Christ as the only revelation of God—and the one-sided concentration on the church that results—are plainly products of one and the same period; both, moreover, reflect this common foundation in their construction.

If we try for a moment to free ourselves from this modern view, one with which we have grown up so completely that we scarcely recognize it for what it is, and try to move back to the time when Creation faith functioned, it is not hard to see the interplay and harmony between the two accents of which we have spoken. God is creating *now;* the life that is born and grows is his work. He has not established the church or sent Christ into the world to *keep up* this bodily life. Moreover, there is a "civil" order that exists independent of the church. And when Luther says that "reason" is to reign there, he intends all the forces for the maintenance of life against death that function in man as man—independent of the preaching of the Gospel—to be included in the term. The desire to care for one's offspring belongs there; so does the

attraction to the opposite sex; and the unwillingness to
expose one's intimate life to strangers. All these things
belong to "reason" and "law."

The problem is that we also have destructive forces
within ourselves. These are death and guilt. Jesus Christ
was sent to overcome these destructive forces that are also a part of life. His victory over them is now proclaimed
by the Gospel. Moreover, this is a subject different from
the one we have just been treating. In any case, it is
only from this other perspective that "the earth" or "the
world" is to be transformed into "the kingdom on the left
hand of God."[75]

In Creation God gives us external, bodily life and
work. The basics we need in order to live rather than
perish can never be won in any other way than by "the
sweat of one's brow." The compulsion exercised by worldly laws also belongs to what is indispensable for the
continuation of life. Compulsion is something the Creator
desires; anarchy is something he abhors. But what has
actually happened in the human "dominion" over the resources of nature that is characteristic of our western
industrial community is that precisely all obstacles to
human activity have been removed except *one*: that limit
is the fact that what gives profit and increases economic
growth must not be stopped. Except for this one limita-
tion which the play of economic forces imposes, western
society is, in principle, anarchical.

This anarchy is aggravated by the fact that the social democracies have accepted the competition among
the free economic powers; they simply interfere to the
extent necessary to ensure that profits are reasonably
distributed. According to this ideology of distribution
the manufacturer, the owner of capital, should not be

allowed to keep all of the surplus that production yields;
employed laborers should be given part of the profit. A
great many terms that nowadays are slogans of every democratic movement illustrate the ideals of this ideology:
the production produces a profit; the profit is a "common
good" that should be divided, and the goal of the distribution of these goods is "welfare for all" or "increase
of the standard of living for all groups." The assumption
is clear: nature has unlimited patience; nature eternally
gives all that we want; and our freedom in relation to the
passive, silent and compliant raw material of the creation
is an unbounded freedom.

This is the point where Gogarten is wrong. He assigns *freedom* the wrong place.[76] This is also the point
at which Ole Jensen in his great work of 1975 expresses
his criticism of "secular theology." In a smaller book
with the title *Under the Power of Economic Growth,* Jensen
expands on his criticism of this theology. Among other
things he sharply attacks Harvey Cox's *The Secular City*
(New York, 1966).[77] According to Jensen, we do *not* have
freedom vis-á-vis nature. Nature is *not* passive and
patient, but resists our exploitation of it. And above
all it "hits back" and hurts us if our ravaging becomes
too thoughtless. To Jensen this means that *the Creator*
"hits back." His Law grows out of Creation, and in the
Law—in the compulsion and restrictions that surround and
protect nature—always lies, at least potentially, an element of "wrath."

In his day Gogarten set the concept of "secularism"
in opposition to the concept of "secularization." According to Gogarten, secularization and the desacralization
of nature through which man was given freedom vis-á-vis
his environment was the contribution of Christianity to

mankind. This freedom was based on faith in the Creator and as long as faith in God was still alive man was free in his relation to the world, because the world did not appear to be all that is. This freedom was, however, hard to preserve when faith in God disappeared. What Gogarten calls "secularism" is an attitude that is unfree because the world that surrounds man has now become everything that is.[78] Note that the concept of God that lies behind these distinctions is one of a transcendent God who is elevated above and separated from his created world, and therefore not present in the things which surround us.

The God of the Bible by contrast *is* present in his world; he makes himself known in the inescapable form of life itself. It is the main thesis of K. E. Løgstrup that everything alive "has form" already and is therefore not simply amorphous raw material waiting for a shape and pattern that man will confer upon it. According to Løgstrup, man cannot live as man if he refuses to show respect for the "form" that the creation around him already has, a form which is prior to all culture. The Law of God is at work all around us and if we obey it, it is life-building. If, however, we expand and grow recklessly at the expense of our surroundings, it punishes. Hence, according to Løgstrup, we never have a total and unlimited freedom vis-á-vis the world. It is true that we can have such freedom, but only through the Gospel which directs us to a kingdom other than the one on earth. Only the Gospel, therefore, holds the promise of unlimited freedom.[79]

I have now arrived at a point in my exposition where it will be necessary to explain the title of this section. The title contains four substantives: "Creation,

Law, Gospel, Church." These four substantives are, moreover, exactly in the order in which they appear in the
titles of my books, namely *Creation and Law* (Swedish,
1958) and *Gospel and Church* (Swedish, 1960). Already in
the preface of the first book I informed my readers that
the next book would follow shortly.[80]

Actually, the two books are a single book conceived
as a unity and laid out with headings that correspond
throughout, with one another. Fortunately the two volumes were published close together and in the correct
chronological order in English. *Creation and Law* appeared in 1961; *Gospel and Church* in 1964.[81] Of special
importance is the parallelism between what is said of
"Man in Creation" at the beginning of the first volume
and of "Man in the Church" at the end of the second.

It may perhaps seem trivial and overly explicit to
stress the inner unity between these two books, but I
have found that excessive explicitness on this point is
needed. Through the years I have discussed the content
of these two books with many people and I have seldom met
anyone who has noticed the *unity* of all that is said in
the two volumes.[82] Only technical matters having to do
with publication compelled me to publish two books instead of one. In light of the subject matter, it would
have been better if everything had been published in a
single continuous work, as it had been written.

As I said above, the unity of "man in Creation" and
"man in the Church" is of special importance. In both
cases the same human being is the object of concern. The
Gospel and Baptism, *not* the specifically established ecclesiastical offices of the church order, are constitutive
of the church. The members of this church are the baptized people who believe in the word and live their

everyday lives in the world. Man in Creation works for
his bread, and, in some form or other, always feels compulsion in his work. He has no possibility of escaping
from the world and establishing some church in isolation
from the conditions of earthly labor. If the religious
person attempts this and begins to build walls around the
church, he thereby destroys the profound solidarity of
that which connects the body of Christ with mankind as a
whole. The Gospel frees the man of faith, but this freedom exists in a body that serves the neighbor and exists
in a creation where work and compulsion still constitute
inescapable conditions built into the structure of society.[83]

It has become difficult for modern post-Enlightenment generations to envision how the creative activity of
God can work through our ordinary laws, laws that are
sometimes, we think, good, and are other times bad. We
alter these laws at regular intervals through fairly
trivial processes of decision in parliaments and congres-
ses. If we find it difficult to link our thoughts about
"God" to this, it is because in our minds we do not generally link the creative work of God with *anything* that
is ordinary, everyday, changeable and non-religious.
With a healthy and living faith in Creation, however, it
should be a simple matter to link God with societal laws.
For in our time it may rightly be asserted that the laws
of society are those entities which, urgently and persistently, remind us of the existence and needs of our
fellowman. The content of the Law of God is, according
to the Bible, love for our neighbor.

Through the Law God performs two different actions:
he compels and he accuses. In both, God desires to bring
about good over against evil. Specifically, through the

Law God seeks to oppose evil and to promote good in a
human who does not freely desire the good. In spite of
this inability to desire the good, however, the human
being is, and remains, a creature of God. This creature-
liness manifests itself in the fact that, in spite of his
opposition, the human being cannot avoid being spontaneously drawn into love and trust for others. Therefore
the compulsion of the Law never means just compulsion.
There remains in man just so much insight into what a
free man could be that he, on the one hand in slavery,
admits his guilt and, on the other hand in the image of
Christ in the Gospel, recognizes his freedom. This compulsion that work lays upon us was called in the sixteenth
century "the civil or political use of the law" (*usus
civilis* or *usus politicus legis*).

In what follows we will consciously hold together
two entities that at first glance seem entirely different:
the Law, which is often spoken of in the singular in the
Bible, and the laws that are in force in earthly society.
The connection between "the Law" and "the laws" is our
fellowman or our "neighbor." In two passages the
Bible sums up "the Law" as love of our neighbor; the laws
of society may in turn be seen as "nagging" and pressing
reminders to us of our fellowmen. It fits well with the
picture of God as the one who creates anew that the laws
change and are perishable.

In two places in the New Testament the Law, then,
is summed up in a single commandment: "You shall love
your neighbor as yourself" (Rom. 13:9 and Gal. 5:14). It
has often been observed that the commandment of love for
our fellowman is not specific to the teaching of Jesus
but has its parallels outside of Christianity. However,
the fact that the commandment exists does not therefore

mean that perfect obedience to the commandment exists.
Paul, who is of the view that the Gentiles "do by nature
what the Law requires" and thereby "are a law to themselves" (Rom. 2:14), never said that the Gentiles are
free from fault. On the contrary, there are many statements about them, in close connection with the passage
about the Law, that give a bleak picture of moral conditions in the Roman Empire outside of Israel (Rom. 1:18-
32).[84]

      This agrees well with our other observations: the
existence of laws in a certain place is often related to
the existence there of law-breaking. But we are not
interested in judging human excellence. Through an analysis of the Creation, we already know, according to Løgstrup, that what supports life, namely, the sovereign manifestations of life, is visible precisely because there
exist forces which destroy life; the two opposed phenomena
of support and destruction exist side by side, even within
the same person. What *is* interesting to us is the role of
our fellowman in this scheme. For the Bible places the
fellowman in a key position. His need for help is God's
own cry to us. It is a cry that summons to action and
therefore a commandment, or law, or "influence in a certain direction," as it is sometimes described in modern
social psychology.

      This means three closely related things. First,
it becomes quite preposterous to try to extract, from
the Bible, a specifically Christian ethos which contains
patterns for actions toward our neighbor in the present
time. Our fellowman himself, in a particular situation,
at a particular moment, makes his needs apparent and real
to us. We do not have to learn from the Bible what he
needs. Second, our fellowman, like ourselves, is both

exposed to that which is good in life and subject to destructive desires. Therefore, in his cry to us, which we
necessarily hear simply by virture of being related to
him, there must be included things that we should resist;
that is, there may be certain things which he desires of
us that we, from our point of view, believe are not in his
best interest. No one, however, can sift and separate the
one from the other without the risk of making mistakes.
Third, while listening to the wishes of our fellowmen, we
always waver between the external compulsion to do a certain
action and the free spontaneity that often causes us to
act before we reflect. "The conscience" is that entity
which generally judges *post facto* an action that one has
just performed without premeditation.

But the call to love our fellowman is greatly complicated by the large number of fellowmen we have who
often have tremendously varying needs. The most ordinary
way of failing a fellow creature is not by directing some
malevolent action toward him, but by simply neglecting
his needs in caring for some other, closer neighbor. Therefore, according to the New Testament, the judgment on the
last day will be severest on those actions we have left
undone (Mt. 25:45).

Two clear examples ought to put an end to any notion
that the ethical contribution of Christianity consists in
the proclamation of a law or requirement that is unknown
to mankind apart from Christ.

The Pharisees knew well the commandment to love
one's neighbor. No one at that time had to hear it from
Jesus. The rich young man, for example, knew it already
in his heart beforehand (Mt. 19:20). Nevertheless, according to Jesus, the pious legalists of those days disregarded their own beloved commandment. The Pharisees,

for example, shut certain people out of the fellowship.
Moreover, they shut out those who needed it most and who
also, according to Jesus, were nearest to the kingdom of
God (Mk. 2:15-17). The fact that the commandment was
given in a formulated sentence did not help those who
knew the Law to discover their fellowman.

The conditions within the Christian congregation
after the death of Jesus reveal the same characteristics.
The congregation not only had the formulated sentence
about loving one's neighbor, but also the clear pictures
of how Jesus realized the command. Yet there was in Cor-
inth exactly the same type of neglect as in ancient Israel.
The fellowship was closed and hence the poor and hungry
person who needed it the most was shut out (I Cor. 11:20-
22). Not even the picture of Christ before the eyes of
the assembled could help them discover their fellowman.
That is why the Law as *compulsion* is necessary.

Isolated passages from the biblical texts and from
later Reformation documents have sometimes been interpreted in such a way that the compulsion of the Law is
thought to be in force outside of the congregation of
Christ, among those who do not sincerely believe, and that
Christians, by contrast, spontaneously keep the command-
ments in undisturbed peace without Law or compulsion. But
this is a misinterpretation of both the Bible and these
Reformation documents. Such antinomian movements are
found throughout ecclesiastical history, but they lie outside the mainstream of Christianity. A more generally
accepted Christian doctrine is that God's compelling Law
is necessary if our fellowman is to receive his due.[85]
Note that the civil use of the law presupposes that the
law compels in the face of opposition from the hearts of
those who obey it.

Since Christians are tempted to select who their
fellows are, thus, in effect, rejecting others, it is possible to say of the legislation of earthly society that
by it the welfare of those whom Christians did not select
is looked after. That is the reason society's laws are
experienced as compulsory. Their paragraphs are our neglected fellowman's dunning letters. When the *really* neglected are protected by the laws, it becomes meaningful
to say that these earthly laws are expressions of God's
Law. The actual laws of a society may, however, sometimes favor groups other than the truly neglected and
thereby, actually foster greater neglect instead of service.

The fact that the laws of a society can be altered
makes new creation for the good of our fellowmen possible.
The continuous new creation of the Creator is not restricted to what Løgstrup calls the sovereign and spontaneous
manifestations of Life, that is, the good we experience
here on earth. God creates afresh even in hard and seem-
ingly inhuman legislation, and thus even in the midst of
compulsion.

Since every human bears within himself the risk of
falling prey to his own or "closed" manifestations of life,
that is, his own destructive desires, society is best ordered when as many people as possible can make their voices
heard and so remind the other members of what is reasonable.
From the point of view of our fellowmen, this is the advantage of democracy. When all have power, each person
with his right to vote has very little power to misuse.
In those types of government in which an individual or an
elite governs, even a relatively minor deviation among
these few has disastrous consequences for many people.
However, such reasoning is one-sided insofar as it

assumes that the greatest need exists *within* the country
in which democratic voting takes place and that the major
problem is therefore the just distribution of resources
among the citizens of that country. However, the development of our society has shown us that technology, industrialization, and demographic changes and their consequent
problems generally cause new needs to arise where old ones
are met. As a result, the problem of finding a reasonable
distribution of resources within any country always remains
unresolved. Despite this fact, however, democracies are—
from an ethical point of view—relatively free from problems.

It is, however, possible that a situation can arise
in which the problem of distribution is so narrowly defined that the attention directed toward one's own country
blurs the issue; that is, a disguised nationalism arises
which actually prevents the just distribution of resources
on a much larger level. This happens, for instance, when
the division between rich and poor within one's own country is not nearly as great as that between rich and poor
nations. If one is poor in Uganda or in the Sudan, a
reasonable economic distribution is not brought about by
democratically conducted parliamentary elections in Sweden
or Canada. Furthermore, reasonable distribution is not
even brought about by democratically conducted elections
in African states themselves, for they have no distribut-
able resources.

This unjust distribution has become a pressing ethical problem for all of Christianity during the latter part
of the twentieth century. The reason for this is simple:
the epoch of colonialism ended after World War II, and
politically independent African and Asiatic states began
to establish themselves right and left. At that time, it

became plain that the political independence of the new
states would be a chimera as long as they lacked economic
independence. It also soon became plain that they would
not attain economic independence without a corresponding
economic disadvantage from European and American business
interests. The opposition between North and South has
thus more or less succeeded the older tension between
East and West.

If it is reasonable to assume that the legislation
of a country represents the "dunning letters" of our fellowmen—the dunning letters of those in need to those who
possess and are strong—then it is the situation today
that the dunning letters which emanate from the southern
hemisphere in the conflict between poor and rich countries
do not, on the whole, reach the privileged in the northern
hemisphere: legislation has not been passed. East and
West, though governed by different economic systems, have
demonstrated remarkably similar attitudes in the face of
current threats from the South, for all have hitherto only
come to their own defense. Probably the church communities, if they are able to assert a biblical view of God's
Law and the laws of the land, have a pioneer task before
them with regard to this issue. International ecumenical
organs have for several years directed their attention to
the problems of Africa and Asia.

However, the legislation of a country does not deal
only with economic distribution, although to an increasing
degree this issue determines the outcome of elections in
democratic states. Rather, each of the laws that govern
people's work and education, the treatment of the sick,
and the exploitation of the environment is a particular
instance of the pressure on all inhabitants of the country
to act in such a way that others will be benefitted.

Therefore, all laws must be changeable, since destruction
is continually taking on new forms and must thus be met
with new laws. The idea that a law is somehow holy if it
is unchangeable contradicts the fundamental thesis of
Creation faith, namely, that "to create is to be continually making anew."

When someone uses the word "law" today, nearly all
listeners immediately think of an unchanging state, one
which maintains the status quo. In the sixteenth century,
by contrast, people would have thought of *movement* when
they heard the word. They would have thought of the then
current dissolution of European patriarchalism and the
parallel establishment of free and worldly states, as well
as the continuously new ventures in practically all fields
taking place within these states. Luther says explicitly
that the Law must be "adapted to the situation" and that
love is sovereign with respect to all laws. If we utilize
Luther at this point, we would think in terms of *opposing*
the status quo to the law! For in Luther the laws represent the mobility of the community.[86]

There are many ways in which "law" tends to become
associated with rigidity and invariability. The doctrine
of Creation which prevailed in Europe, especially in Germany, a generation ago, presupposes what Luther opposes,
namely that God's work of Creation took place "in the beginning" and that God, therefore, was once upon a time a
Creator but is now something else, that is, a Savior.
As a result of his actions in the beginning, according to
this static way of thinking, there are now certain ordi-
nances on earth (*Schöpfungsordnungen*). In contrast, when
Luther explains in his *Smaller Catechism* what "heaven and
earth" mean in the First Article of the Creed, he never
once mentions either the word "heaven" or "earth," but

says instead: "God has created me...." Every birth, then, is a creation; God creates even *now*.

A development away from mobility has also taken place within Catholic theology. Just as Confessional Lutheranism, after the Enlightenment and the Romantic Movement, was driven into maintaining the value of the existing order first against the impulses of the French Revolution, and then against the impulses of Marxism, so the church of Rome was opposed to the whole direction in which nineteenth century society went. The concept of "natural law" (*lex naturalis*) was consequently inter-preted in the same way as the concept of the *Schöpfungs-ordnungen* in Protestantism: that is, the right to owner-ship was asserted and reasonable land reforms were re-jected. The interpretation, then, favored the status quo and the ideal of immobility.

This distorted view of Creation and Law is finally in the process of being swept aside in both Protestantism and Catholicism. For one thing, the doctrine of Creation is once again being reasonably interpreted, for renewed criticism is being leveled at ecclesiastical authorities who use the idea of a natural law in a one-sidedly con-servative way. This is especially true in the area of sexual morality; several Catholic theologians have recent-ly rejected papal theses on the right of the church to control the free decisions of people.[87] Seen in a larger perspective, this means two things. First, "law" is now more strongly associated with "Creation," especially with new Creation. Second, the Law has thereby become a *mobile* entity rather than a rigid and invariable one.

From this it is clear that no Law is eternal. God's Law is God's because it is changeable. If it were un-changeable, it could not be God's, for it would then

nullify the idea that God is the Creator *now*. God continuously undertakes new actions as destruction continuously appears in new forms. Old laws still in force are
an excellent tool for the ethical egoist: if he searches
long enough, he finds loopholes through which he can acquire advantages for himself, thereby depriving his fellowman of his due. When the God of the Decalogue creates,
he reveals hidden murders and legal thefts. He builds
new barriers against shrewdness and, with the help of his
Law gives freedom to the oppressed. The Law of God that
is then established through societal laws will, however,
eventually again be utilized for destruction and must,
therefore, be continuously re-evaluated on the basis of
love for the neighbor.

     But if the idea that "no law is external" were to
have only this meaning, it would be banal. The idea becomes more controversial, however, when it is taken to
mean that the Law is an instrument of God only in *this*
life, only here and now. It is important to emphasize
this in the face of one of the long-standing consequences
of the Platonic idea of the existence of a spiritual and
material world; that is, the tendency to see the Law as
it functions on earth as a reflection of an everlasting,
constant and unchangeable Law. Biblical evidence for
this kind of view is very difficult to find. For since
the Law is a divine work with human beings who do not
freely and spontaneously will what God wills, a set of
terms other than those associated with the Law is used in
the Bible to describe eternal life; namely "freedom,"
"salvation," and "song of praise." The thought that
eternal life involves man's adaption to an eternal Law
is one alien to scripture.

     Now, this does not mean that what the Law demands

should be absent from the realm of freedom and praise.
On the contrary, the Law itself demands something, which,
were it realized, would abrogate the Law as Law. That
is, it demands that life be allowed to manifest itself
freely, and therefore requires, paradoxically, its own
disappearance. Throughout the history of the church, all
interpreters of scripture who have rejected the doctrine
of "the third use of the Law," have done so because they
wished to defend a Law so severe, in the sense mentioned
above, that it *must* disappear. In contrast, those who
have desired to make use of the idea of "the third use of
the Law" have done so because they were fearful of the
careless and egoistic freedom that might ensue if, in the
Christian doctrine, there were included ideas about man's
freedom from the Law.

   The scandal of Jesus and his preaching lay chiefly
in the fact that he lacked any such fear. His sermon in
the synagogue of Nazareth (Lk. 4:16-21) demonstrates a
clear conflict not only with the Jewish misinterpretation
of the Old Testament Law, but also with the Law itself.
The Gospel of Jesus abolishes the judgment of God's own
Law on the sinner.[88] Therefore, those interpreters of
the Bible who emphasize the conflict between Law and Gospel are more in line with primitive Christianity than
those who stress the harmony of the two. The Law is not
an end in itself, but rather, the goal of salvation is
freedom from the Law, and hence the song of praise. On
this point Paul represents a more radical form of Christianity than the other primitive Christian authors, for
in Paul "freedom"—not chiefly "obedience"—becomes the
main word.

   It is natural for those who deny that the Law is
eternal to believe that the Law has an accusing function.

But the Law has this function only up to a certain point;
after that, the Gospel, which is the Law's opposite, takes
over.   However, if one believes that the end of everything
is the willing and obedient subjection of man to the Law,
then the accusing function of the Law is softened, and it
becomes an eternal Law.   This was the prevailing view of
Law in ancient Israel, as the 119th Psalm, for example,
indicates.

Using traditional technical terms, we can express
the attitudes of the different Christian communities toward the Law in the following ways: where obedient submission to the Law is thought to be what God intends for his
creatures, there the "third use of the Law" will be most
important.   Where the Law is seen as accusing and judging,
there the "second use of the Law" will be given priority.
Integral to this latter view are two emphases: the demand
for freedom, which is the opposite of compulsion, and the
belief in the ability of the Gospel, in bringing about
freedom, to have an ethically regenerating and joyous effect without the Law.

Calvin is a good representative of the doctrine of
the "third use of the Law," and Luther of the Law's muta-
bility and the freedom of the Gospel.   Both have followers
on the secular level.   Kant's dream of a republic governed
by "respect for the law" is a parallel to Calvin; the
Marxist dream of "a classless society" characterized by
spontaneous playfulness resembles Luther's eschatology.

When the life that is brought about by the resurrection from the dead is distinguished by freedom rather than
obedience to an eternal law, this life is being described
according to the picture that Jesus Christ paints in his
death and resurrection.   For he was condemned and suffered
and died under the Law (Rom. 8:3, Gal. 4:4, 2 Cor. 5:21);

it was for him something harsh. Living life through
faith in him means, therefore, living in fellowship with
him, here in the world of work and compulsion, as we
await freedom.

It is finally possible at this point in my analysis to draw together here a few disconnected threads that
have been left hanging in the various sections. One such
thread is from the section II called "Before Basel," in
which I attempted to get back to the classical periods
before the Enlightenment. I there treated Irenaeus under
the heading "Salvation Means Becoming Human Again" (section II.a). Worth noting about the Irenaean view of salvation is the absence of any "addition" to what is human.
For Irenaeus salvation is, quite simply, becoming human
again. "Recapitulation" (salvation) is living the life
of Creation, that is, the self-denying life that Jesus
lived, for it is *this* life that he crowned with resurrection. He is as yet alone in having been raised, but
through Baptism, which is death and resurrection, he now
draws mankind into the same resurrection that he himself
has already won. This is freedom and the song of praise.

Luther made the next contribution: "Faith Lives in
the World" (section II.b). A dimension introduced during
the Reformation—new, relative to the Church Fathers—was
the strong stress on earthly life as life under the *Law*,
that is, life spent in work for the sake of our neighbor.
This earthly life is good since it sustains God's created
world and gives well-being to those who surround us. But
it does *not* make man righteous before God. Moreover, *all*
lives lived under the Law, whether those of Christians or
non-Christians, have this sustaining effect. The same is
true of the social contributions of the church; these
"contributions"—which in the ecumenical debate of our

time often function to "justify" the church as an institution—would be just as useful if some institution other
than the church contributed them. For good deeds done in
the earthly realm benefit their recipient regardless of
who does them. With tremendous consistency Luther viewed
life on earth as life without any religious decorations.

This is most clearly seen in his doctrine of "the
highest purpose of the Law," that is, the use of the Law
which accuses the conscience and condemns man before God.
The Law *kills* and *crucifies* when it fulfills this purpose;
that is to say, the Law itself "empties" man of divine
life and makes him a "sinner." This is also called the
"spiritual use of the Law" (*usus spiritualis legis*).[89]
Thus, the death and resurrection which Baptism represents
are fulfilled in the banality of everyday work—where, at
each moment, we experience the Law's compulsion—with its
total lack of religious overtones. Christ is closest to
man in that which, from the vantage point of "religious
experience," appears to be most insignificant.

Therefore everything depends on faith. To have
faith is to defy what the eyes see and the other senses
perceive. And this defiance is "the beginning of the resurrection of the dead."

Gospel and Freedom

Among those who emphasize Creation and the First
Article today, the accent on the Gospel and the Second
Article is usually weak. But this imbalance is peculiar
to our time; during the struggle of the Church Fathers
against the Gnostics, for example, an equally strong accent was placed on the two points that we today are inclined to separate, namely, the theses that God has created
matter and that salvation is the resurrection of the dead.

In the early church the element which unified these theses was "matter," which God, according to the Gnostics,
could not have created and could not possibly wish to
save from destruction. In the context of this struggle
the church composed its Trinitarian Creed, stressing
first the Creation of "heaven and earth" and placing at
the end "the resurrection of the body and the life everlasting." In between is the center of it all: Christ,
the Word become "flesh," that is, the Word that became
material and that was raised from the dead on the third
day.

I n our time the Danish theological tradition following Grundtvig is of special interest, for in it the
Church Fathers of the second century, especially Irenaeus,
become alive again. At the same time, because of its
radically new approach, Danish theology has good contact
with the interpretation of human life offered by contemporary philosophy, literature and theater. In light of
Denmark's theological wealth, it is strange to see American translators and publishers of theological literature
paying attention to West German authors of fairly limited
interest while ignoring a theologian and religious philosopher like Løgstrup. At this point in my analysis, I find
that it is more important to come to terms with Løgstrup
than to take up any other European. But because this
Dane is relatively unknown, I will first briefly give an
account of certain of his fundamental thoughts, among
which the central two are the doctrines of Creation and
eschatology.[91]

I should point out that the reason for my inclusion
of a somewhat more explicit description of Danish theology
in this section on "Gospel and Freedom" rests on the fact
that the main thesis of the finished section on "Creation

and Work" is that Christian life is, as to its content, secular life. Not even Bonhoeffer stressed this thesis as strongly as has K. E. Løgstrup. With regard to the resurrection (both the kerygma of the resurrection of Christ and the promise of our own resurrection), which is the core of the Gospel from the vantage point of this thesis, much modern theology seems to constitute an anti-mythological fleeing from the body. Even theologians who otherwise readily speak of the body, of society, and of matter ("the material conditions") suddenly become inclined to flight from Creation when the resurrection is mentioned.

But I have not fled. On the contrary, years ago I was fascinated by "the resurrection of the body." Already in *The Living Word* (1949) there are explicit analyses of the theme of "the necessity of the body," and in *Credo* (1974) the section on the resurrection is one of the most "scandalous" parts of the whole book. The offense appears more serious if one considers the fact that I normally readily engage in demythologization. The story of the Creation in Genesis, just like the story of the ascension in Luke and in Mark, must, according to my view, be demythologized if its real meaning for our time is to be seen. But if bodiliness is taken out of the resurrection, then bodiliness disappears in the interpretation of Baptism and the Holy Communion as well. And this disappearance has devastating consequences for one's view of the relation of church and world.[92]

Løgstrup's main thesis concerning the relationship of Creation and Gospel is most clearly seen in his discussion of the distinction between "the universal" and "the specific" in the Christian faith. On the one hand, according to Løgstrup, God is active in all the processes

which humans perceive and in which they have a part. On
the other hand, there is the Gospel concerning one unique
event that is tied to the one concrete historical person
Jesus. In Løgstrup's view,the universal, which we
all experience and receive, may be spoken of on the basis
of experiences that are common to all mankind. The Bible
contains very clear statements about these general human
experiences. But everything is turned upside down when
we assert that mankind can discover God's universal work
only on the basis of the biblical text. When we come to
the resurrection, however, we realize that we could never
construct the Gospel from our general human experience if
the event were not recorded in a historical report.

As regards the *Gospel* (the specific) then, we are
dependent on a certain limited group of people who are
able to tell us of the unique thing that happened at a
particular point in history. The narrative is the kerygma
(the Second Article of Faith). We cannot construct the
Gospel out of experience simply because of the fact that
general human existence is ambiguous. That is, though
life contains the gift of processes and manifestations
which support and sustain human existence, it also contains events and manifestations which are a threat to all
human life and whose whole direction is destruction. Each
kind of manifestation is, however, equally real. Moreover, the two are not similar in any sense at all. It is,
then, according to Løgstrup, not possible for us to give
a univocal interpretation of life. Against any talk of
the power for good, many examples of actual cruelty can
always be given—even of cruelty that is adopted, successful, and never questioned.

Given what we know of life's ambiguity, it would
not then appear improbable that perfect goodness without

destruction or the desire to hurt once existed in human
form on earth, and that this very human was executed in
the most cruel way. But the story of Jesus' life and
death culminates in *Easter*——the story of his resurrection, the event which is the core of the Gospel. And
this human being, the one who gives only life and not
destruction, *lives at this very moment,* and is close to
those who in faith reach out toward him. This specific
word, that is, the Gospel, cannot be made probable or
plausible on the basis of general human experience. It
remains a word at the edge of our human existence, pointing beyond, to "another kingdom." But the Gospel does
have a life-building function which it can fulfill here
and now: it can support the will to live in a person who,
assailed on all sides by destruction, yet deep in his
soul ardently longs for life, love and hope.

Faith, then, can be built on the basis of general
human experience, but it will always be a faith that is
threatened and so cannot survive without being given
support. The Gospel of Jesus Christ has for generations
been just such a life-support. But this Gospel cannot
today build life against destruction if what we call "the
universal" (faith in life as a gift) is judged to be something quite impossible, that is, lacking any foundation
in *general* human experience. This thesis that faith in
the Creator lacks "natural" support within our lives and
can only be found in the revelation of the Bible is nihilistic——it destroys faith. On the basis of this thesis,
which is, of course, Barth's famous negative thesis and
the foundation of his purely Christological system, the
Gospel can never be anything other than a demand for
blind submissiveness to a written authority. Such submissiveness is not faith, however, but is itself, in

spite of all its words about Jesus, nihilism.[93]

In order that the Gospel might have meaning for the human who hears its "specific" word, man's universal interpretation of life, based on experience common to all, must contain faith. When Løgstrup describes this constantly threatened faith which seeks support, I myself always see the picture of a New Testament situation. For example, two Gentiles who are described in the New Testament as examples of "faith," namely the Roman officer of Matthew 8:10 and the Cannanite woman of Matthew 15:28, are representative of the people outside Israel who present a picture of "faith." And their faith, observable (in its external aspect) to the eye, is based on a *general human need* (Mark 1:24). In our post-Enlightenment era, anchoring Christian faith in the generally human is, according to Løgstrup, more necessary than it ever has been before.

Moreover, this anchoring in the generally human must take place in a much more radical form than ever before. For before the Enlightenment, the term "God" belonged to ordinary usage, and it did not mean blind submission to some authority. Ecclesiastical authorities demanded assent to dogmas *about* God, and there were different dogmas in different church denominations, but the word "God" was a part of everyday language, something it is not today. Therefore it is important in the present time to analyze human life in such a way that every human being, including the atheist, discovers "the universal" according to Christian faith in his everyday experience. If what is in accord with Christian faith is really universal, then it is to be found in the experience of every human being.

If the Creator is at this very moment creating

newness and life in the earthly life of every human being,
which is what the Christian claims in assenting to the
First Article of Faith, then every human being, in looking about, must be able to discover *gifts* in his life;
that is, things which he cannot create himself but must
be *given* to him. Equally inevitably, the human being,
in looking about, discovers the opposite phenomenon,
namely, the universal principle of destruction in our
lives that deprives us of life and constitutes a threat
to our trust. For human life contains both new Creation
and destruction. And both are apprehensible prior to the
Gospel. For Jesus acted precisely in this world characterized by ambiguity when he entered the life of mankind.
He is, according to the Gospel, our "savior," because he
placed himself on the side of life over against death:
he healed the sick, he restored sinners, and he was resurrected on the third day. The character of salvation
becomes incomprehensible if this "doubleness" of life is
not a given *prior to* the Gospel.

This ambiguity is, however, not a property of life
apart from ourselves. *We* are involved in matters that
build up the lives of others; *we* are involved in matters
that destroy other people's lives. In this context Løgstrup presents his analysis of the so-called "sovereign
and closed manifestations of life," as he calls them.
Trust, love, and sincerity are sovereign; that is, they
are not reactions to what others have done to us but are
free and total. Therefore they open up new possibilities
of life around us. And, according to Løgstrup, they are
always *given*. If our will to live is broken, we cannot,
through a moral decision, create trust, love, and sincerity toward those around us. Moreover, if these positive
manifestations of life return, they return because they

are again *given* to us in the same way as life itself is
given.

Hatred, mistrust, and insincerity are, in contrast,
reactions; that is, they are by nature secondary and derived. They do not open up but rather close down the
possibilities of life for people around us. And they
are—purely linguistically—impossible to describe in
positive terms: it is necessary to use negative formula-
tions in order to describe them at all. Everyday language
has no description free of evaluations of love and hatred,
or of trust and mistrust, for this process of evaluation
is included in the very way in which ordinary language
designates certain manifestations of life. According to
Løgstrup, it is simply not possible to avoid such evaluation if we want to use ordinary, everyday language.[94]
Science and contemporary philosophy, however, seek to
separate evaluation from the description of facts; consequently the fundamental manifestations of everyday life
simply do not become the subjects of analysis.

Instead, contemporary philosophy limits itself to
an analysis of those human conditions in which man determines the situation by voluntary decisions and acts. Such
decisions and acts are, indeed, important. But they are
not the acts that sustain and develop human life. Without
the sovereign manifestations of life—love, trust, mercy—
over which man exercises no disposal but which are *given*
to him, all human life would be lost.

Even though spontaneous love and benevolence may
be absent, it does not therefore follow that all moral
behavior is bad. Some forms of external moral behavior
are "good" even though they be "forced." Bringing up
children and legislation are two examples of the way in
which these acts and what earlier theologians called "the

civil use of the law" (*usus civilis legis*) all rest on
moral decisions.

But the source of the Law is "Creation." For the
sovereign manifestations of life are the works of the
Creator underway in the givens of life now. But constantly God must create anew in conflict with the opposing
closed manifestations of life in order to prevent their
triumph. This, then, is "Law."

It is typical of both the sovereign and the closed
manifestations of life that they seize man; Luther would
have said man is "ridden" by them. (According to Luther,
God and the Devil are two beings who alternately take man
in their power and "ride" him.)[95] For Løgstrup it is
crucial that theology and philosophy present, as far as
possible, a purely *phenomenological* analysis of how this
seizure takes place. The words "God" and "Devil" should
not be used in the course of the analysis, for it is in
ordinary secular life without any articulated religious
dimension that one finds the arena in which God and the
Devil struggle with one another.

The Gospel is now spoken to this secular existence.
What do the Gospel's words about "freedom" mean? What is
meant by "resurrection from the dead"? According to Løgstrup, the answer to those questions is complicated by
our modern insight into the meaningless cruelty of nature,
as, for example, in earthquakes and other catastrophes,
and by our post-Darwinian insight into the planned and
"meaningful" cruelty of nature. Earlier theology could
link "death" and "sin" together in a way which has become impossible for us. For modern man, dying, conceived
of as the result of an active, process of nature, is
part of creation itself. In this view, then, dying has
nothing to do with *sin*.[96] Therefore, according to Løg-

strup, we can no longer link the victory of the Gospel
over the Law with the victory of life over death.

In Løgstrup's work, the Lutheran opposition between
Law and Gospel tends, therefore, to be an opposition of
peripheral importance. The message of the Gospel concerning resurrection and eternal life is relevant
for us, but relevant only as something that points toward
"another kingdom"—a kingdom different from the one we
now live. That God in forgiveness abolishes his own Law
does not become the essential message of the Gospel.
What is essential is that God now cosmically acts against
his Creation, abolishing, in the resurrection, that *biological*, and therefore inculpable, cruelty built into Creation which is most devastating to our will to live.

In Løgstrup's theology, it is generally true that
the freedom and sovereignty which Christian preaching
traditionally located in faith in Jesus Christ has been
moved into "the sovereign manifestations of life." Freedom and new creation are thus regarded as generally human
manifestations of life (the "universal"), rather than as
belonging to peculiarly "Christian" life (the "specific").
What opens us to a life entirely different from the one
we know and experience in the here and now constitutes,
according to Løgstrup, the unique content of Christianity.

In my views, such an interpretation too weakly accents the freedom given through the Gospel. I believe
that the resurrection of Christ bestows upon the believer
a triumphant sovereignty that extends into the realm of
work and compulsion in the life we live in the here and
now before death.[97]

I believe that the empty tomb on the morning of the
third day is something that is, purely historically speaking, hard to get around. True, it is a painfully physical

story. But if we eliminate the physical, bodily elements
in the text, we create more problems than we solve. About
three things we are historically certain: First, Jesus and
his disciples came from Galilee, and only temporarily
visited Jerusalem. Second, the crucifixion and interment
took place in Jerusalem, a city which was an alien place
for them. Finally, immediately after the execution and
burial the disciples began to preach the resurrection of
Christ, not in Galilee, where they belonged, but in this
alien city so hostile to Jesus.

         This is historically certain. Moreover, it all must
have happened with great speed. After a short time there
were Christian congregations in Antioch and in Damascus,
that is to say, abroad. Exegetes are, as we know, willing
to assent to "visions" in the home district of Galilee,
but they deny the possibility of an empty tomb in Jerusalem. Behind this exegetical consent to the possibility
of purely mental phenomena rather than physical phenomena
and the body lie two silent assumptions: on the one hand,
the common European and fundamentally Platonic contrast
between body and soul and, on the other, an intense personal uneasiness about the relatively common and ordinary
historical descriptions of rumors about an empty tomb.
Some suggest mistakes were made about the place of burial;
others that there was a confusion of dead bodies, perhaps
even a theft. But the most interesting dimension of this
approach is the strange benevolence of the Liberal exegetes
toward believers in existing Christian congregations: they
assume that if we give the mental experiences of apostles
to the church today, we will thereby have given the church
something by which to live.[98]

         It may be suitable at this point to say something
about the earliest Christian congregations of the second

and third centuries. First, however, it is necessary to
distinguish between two kinds of "offense to reason"
which confront us moderns when we stand before the primitive Christian kerygma concerning Jesus. The first and
most serious "offense" confronts us in the form of the
assumption found in the kerygma that the salvation of all
mankind is accomplished through what happened to one
single man of the many men who have lived. This serious
"offense" has, however, been widely accepted wherever the
preaching of Christ is heard. It is accepted uncritically even by those who seek to lessen the offense by limiting the resurrection of this one man to an inward or
mental phenomenon such as the visions of the disciples.
In the second century, for example, "Jesus is Lord" was
an offensive confession.[99]

The second "offense" is more endurable. It consists of the thought that this one man was, on the bodily
level, able to function differently than we do. It is
offensive to assume, for example, that he functions, on
the bodily level, in a unique way in relation to our souls.
However, to experience Jesus' unique functioning on the
bodily level as an "offense" shows a general uneasiness
about the thought of God's being related to the bodily.

It is typical that those theologies that most ener-
getically seek to avoid even touching upon the problem of
the empty tomb are, at the same time, theologies in which
the idea of Creation is absent (i.e., Liberalism and existentialism). In times past it was easier than it is
today to assent to this "offense" concerning bodiliness.

For primitive Christianity, the empty tomb means
nothing without some kind of continuity between Jesus and
the Creation. This does not mean, however, that there is
a belief in the risen Jesus as existing with bodily cells;

he is transformed.   There is no doubt in primitive Christianity about this fact; the visions bear witness to this.
Nonetheless, there is the same kind of continuity between
the crucified Christ and the risen Lord that there is between seed and harvest in I Cor. 15:35-49.   This Jesus
who was the seed now lives among those who believe   in
him as the harvest.   And it is not only the memory of him
that is alive; the outward sign of his continuity was the
empty tomb.

     To be sure, the empty tomb itself awakens no faith
nor provides irrefutable proof—just as buried grains of
wheat cannot in themselves awaken faith.   What is sown
is nothing at all unless the seed is seen to be connected
with a *harvest*; that is, with the life-giving forces that
set in *after* the total sacrifice—the animating forces
that come from Baptism and Holy Communion, from the visions of the disciples, and from Christian fellowship.
What is sown is connected with the harvest in the certainty that all death in Christ is, at bottom, life, even
something more than what reigned before Christ came.   But
if the sown grains, that is, that which cannot in itself
awaken faith, are held together with the harvest, then by
their outwardness,   bodiliness and earthliness, they represent a tremendous asset; they demonstrate that nothing,
however repulsive, can now extinguish hope.

     The cross at Golgotha and the empty tomb give rise
to a confident, free, and unencumbered walk into the future.   This confidence and freedom is a kind of sovereignty in relation to external dangers that the mental experiences or visions alone could never give.   In this combination of Golgotha and Easter lies the key to the unbe-
lievable story of the young church in the Roman Empire,
for the first Christian congregation's affirmation of

the material and physical side of the resurrection fits
perfectly with the strange concentration on the future
which characterized its whole life. Christ was in the
center of whatever the congregation encountered. All
along he was at the vanguard, in the light, at the door-
way opening to the tunnel of suffering. For the young
Christian congregation it was not meaningless to be hung
on a cross or to be driven in among wild beasts in an
arena (I Cor. 15:32) or to be thrown into a grave somewhere in the Roman Empire. It made no difference where
one found oneself, for "we are more than conquerors through
him who loved us" (Rom. 8:37).

Primitive Christian faith was construed in this way.
The axis around which everything turned was Jesus' death
and resurrection.   The ascension was mentioned as a separate event (Mark 16:19f., Luke 24:50f., Acts 1:9), though
neither Matthew nor John relate it. Moreover, it was
originally seen in such a way that the office of the Lord
of Heaven was included in it; the risen Lord of the future
who has been established as a judge with the right to for-
give is "in Heaven" and has the power of God to be everywhere during all days to come (Mark 16:20, Mt. 28:18-20).

Such was the situation in the beginning, historically speaking. Christianity entered the region around the
Mediterranean with a certain set of ideas of which the
crucifixion and the resurrection, both conceived of in a
painfully concrete, bodily way, constituted the center.[100]
All becomes incomprehensible if we eliminate the bodily
dimension.

From what do we as Christian people today draw life?
Perhaps for us the message of the resurrection must be reduced purely to the promise of a different future. Løgstrup emphasizes strongly the modern insight that biotic

processes have a built-in cruelty, an insight which, according to his view, separates us from earlier generations and makes it necessary for us to coordinate Creation and Gospel in a different manner than did previous
generations. If possible, according to Løgstrup, we must
not make death itself into something evil in the ethical
sense.

     As far as older texts are concerned, the New Testa-
ment is not especially bound to the idea that death comes
through sin. Though it is true that this thought is
found there, Jesus utters critical words against every
linkage of present misfortune with past causes. In the
face of physical misfortunes he looks forward: "It was
not that this man sinned, or his parents, but that the
works of God might be made manifest in him" (John 9:3; cf.
Luke 13:2-4).

     It is this *looking forward* that is typical of primi-
tive Christianity: now the physically evil is actually
here; now it is our task in faith to bear what happens
to us; now the resurrected Lord is present among us *in
the midst* of this world of death and compulsion. The cross
of Jesus and all that befalls us are linked together, and
these two realities, separated in time, become *one* reality.
Moreover, what happened to Jesus in the resurrection on
the third day is linked to what will happen to us; we will
receive life through death. These two "resurrections" become *one* reality, held fast in the present and tasted now
in faith.

     It is not at all impossible to feel and sense in our
time this primitive Christian sense of life. Every Christian is offered the same interpretation as earlier generations in what actually happens to him in his own life.
But it is hard to keep this interpretation fresh and alive

if the bodily or the physical is left out of the picture and if it remains unproclaimed, for the freedom and sovereignty of faith is then curtailed. Whatever the empty tomb means (and it has never meant a body walking on the earth now with its own cells as distinct from our cells), faith has the right to interpret everything as having been overcome. The empty tomb represents the struggle of faith for *total* freedom and sovereignty here on *earth*.

We must stress that our concern is freedom and sovereignty, not passive submission to the misfortunes that occur. It is true that Christian talk of "bearing the cross in everyday life" has functioned masochistically. It has driven many individual persons to find unsound pleasure in suffering, especially in those forms of piety in which flight from the world has been conceived as more holy than work in the world. But these religious deviations from the mainstream of Christian faith have lacked a sound and vital belief in the Creator. For it is only when the First Article concerning Creation is a living article of faith that its earthliness lends tone to the Second Article concerning the interpretation of what happened to Jesus; so too with the Third Article and its interpretation of what happens to us now in the church and in the future through death. Nowhere in the Creed can faith abandon the physical and the bodily.[101]

That faith cannot abandon the body means that faith cannot abandon man. In this respect, the idea of the church as "the body of Christ" has been a foundation and a motif-creating factor of exceptional importance in Christian ethics, for it has always most strongly emphasized people and their needs. "Body" in this connection means two things. On the one hand it means the body of

the resurrected Christ.   Christ is alive, and he is *human-*
ly alive, clothed in everyday services of healing, and
satisfying hunger and thirst.   On the other hand, "body"
means the community, with its many different members, in
which the services are performed.   If all the members of
the church performed the same actions, the needs of mankind would never be met; but when the church in its activity is *human*, precisely then its life is a healing sign
of the resurrection of Christ.

These human services take place in a world of sin
and destruction among unliberated people over whom powers
reign that cannot desire liberation for all, since this
liberation would mean losses especially for those who now
exercise the powers of coercion.   That is why "the secular
realm" is the realm of work and compulsion, governed by
laws that are intended to make it reasonably tolerable.
Luther continuously described the world where life should
be lived in this manner: in this earthly realm the Christian is "the freest Lord of everything."   Since in faith
and love he wants to serve his neighbor, he therefore ac-
cepts hard external conditions of his life as the only
arena where his neighbor can be reached.   The world of
work and compulsion is therefore "a free prison" for the
Christian.   Luther's vivid expression of the idea of
Christian sovereignty and freedom is applicable not only
to society in the sixteenth century, but also to that of
the twentieth.   This can be illustrated especially with
examples from Latin America today.[102]

This Christian freedom and sovereignty rests on
the certainty that Christ is arisen and that nothing that
happens can wrest from him his power over the future. In
that unfolding complex of events, around which the Second
Article of the Creed gathers everything, lies a key that

can open up and resolve the complexities of earthly
events in the present. Opposition and defeat can be interpreted through Jesus' death and resurrection as well
as victories and newly won external freedom. Faith meets
nothing that is ultimately disheartening. Everything,
dark experiences as well as light ones, rolls toward a
future of resurrection of life.

What is usually called "the second coming of Christ"
is an element in the Christian faith with which we cannot
part. It is true that the term has generally been used
erroneously by the few apocalyptical groups to which it
is common. The New Testament does not contain the expression "Second Coming";[103] moreover, primitive Christianity
could not have originated the term because Christ as
arisen and alive is the "He that cometh" in every service
and in every Holy Communion. Christ is present among men,
and therefore "coming," in the same way as the sun is active among men because its rays are literally continuously
"coming."[104] Nevertheless, what the term "second coming"
stands for cannot be given up. It is in *the future* that
Christ now lives; it is from the future that he now speaks;
and it is from thence that he "comes."

Christ's arrival in the Last Judgment means that the
world of work and compulsion will then at last be translated into total and unlimited freedom. And this translation and realization will take place through a Man who
is coming, that is, the only Man who has hitherto won total freedom—freedom from death. That humanity through
which the body of Christ is a servant on earth—the congregation—will still be there in the end. Man and the
body are never forsaken.

V. A NEW SITUATION IN EUROPE

It may seem to be a divergence from the method of
exposition hitherto followed that I shall now introduce a to
ic about Europe rather than a topic about my authorship
or a problem of theology. This is, however, not the case.
In two large books from the 1970s (*Växling och kontinuitet*
of 1972 and *Credo* of 1974) I have dealt with the present
break between state and church in Europe. Moreover, as
far as the local Swedish debate is concerned, I have actively taken sides in favor of breaking the present ties.[105]

In my judgment there is a directly relevant theological side to this issue. The Christian faith has never
been formulated in a vacuum. Every situation that has
brought about a closer definition of the content of faith
has had a polemical dimension involving dangers for and
challenges to the faith. For example, the difference between Irenaeus and Luther is ultimately due to the external
historical situation with which each had to deal. Irenaeus
wrote from out of a situation in which the Christian church
was a persecuted minority. By contrast, Luther found himself in a situation in which the church dominated the state
everywhere in Europe. As I have already tried to show,
this difference had a direct and obvious bearing upon how
each described the content of the Christian faith.

Similarly, it is fair to say that the changes now
taking place in Europe play an important role in the way
the churches present their messages today. In the judgment of many reviewers, my publications of the 1970s show
the signs of having been composed in a period different
from my earlier works. It has been said that the voice
of Irenaeus can be heard with increasing clarity whereas
the voice of Luther has become weaker and weaker. I hope
these reviewers are right.

At this point I shall proceed with a brief survey
of the vastly differing characteristics of three important centuries in European history. These centuries are
the fourth, the sixteenth, and the twentieth. In the
fourth century the Emperor consolidated the Roman Empire.
Small city states with their own languages were defeated
militarily and politically. The promised eschatological
peace for which the people had waited, but which had been
hindered by the wars of the many states against one another, was at last realized in the armed peace of the Empire.
Constantine the Great himself interpreted his victory as
the result of divine intervention, and the Christian
church accepted this interpretation. For example, Eusebius supported the Constantinian theory with several biblical arguments. According to Eusebius, the tower of
Babel and the evil division of languages represented the
small states which the Roman Empire had defeated. The
peace that God had promised meant one kingdom, one emperor,
one language, and one religious faith.[106]

The trend of the fourth century was away from independent minor states of great antiquity towards a unified
empire with a single language forced upon its inhabitants.
The church viewed this process as the will of God for mankind. Actually much of what we moderns regard as ecclesiastical and political coercion did not emerge until the
fourth century when the Empire was made uniform through
a centralized system of legislation. Before the time of
Constantine, however, there was considerable pluralism
in the churches' conduct of worship services. For instance, there were different dates for the celebration
of Easter in different parts of the Mediterranean region.
However, after Constantine, Easter was given the fixed
place in the calendar that is considered the only correct

one throughout the western world today. Furthermore, we
can say with great certainty that a strictly regulated
state-church would never have allowed the canonizing of
a Holy Writ in which the life of Jesus is told four times
in four different ways. The four Gospels are manifestations of an original pluralism and freedom in the church.[107]

The Reformation in the sixteenth century claimed to
have recovered the original freedom of the primitive
church. In many points it is undoubtedly the case that
the freedom of primitive Christianity returned in the Reformation. But the freedom possessed by the church before
A.D. 300 to clothe the Gospel in different outward forms
in different parts of the world was not recovered. Instead, after A.D. 1500, state coercion with uniformity in
worship services and doctrine increased. It would be
easy to show historically how small the difference between
Luther and Calvin were in comparison to the much greater
differences that exist within the New Testament. The differences between John and Paul, or between Matthew and
Paul, or between John and Matthew are all much more basic
than the differences that existed between the various reformers of the sixteenth century. In the primitive church
there was no earthly prince to create division and conflict among the different groups and evangelists. The
church endured four evangelists besides Paul.

The Reformation on the other hand was much more a
political phenomenon than the Early Church. Kings and
princes made use of biblical interpretations and theolo-
ies in their actions. When Luther repudiated the earthly
power of the Pope and preached "the independence of the
earthly kingdom from church rulers, he increased the independence not only of those who were already kings, but also

of those who were not yet kings. In the sixteenth
century new nation-states arose in opposition to the idea
of a politically centralized and uniform Europe. This
new trend was diametrically opposed to what had characterized the fourth century. Ironically enough, arguments
from the sphere of scripture were again used; but in the
sixteenth century they were used in favor of political
decisions that totally abolished the uniformity which
was the express and biblically motivated ideal of the
fourth century. Latin had to be removed from the Mass.
As Olaus Petri's introduction to the Swedish Mass of 1531
says: "Vi svenske höre ock Gudi till savä̈l som annor folk.
Han föraktar icke heller mera vart tungomal än annor
tungomal": "We Swedes belong to God just as much as other
peoples. He despises our language no more than other
languages."

Another piece of history also illustrates the point
about the political character of the Reformation. Gustav
Vasa, the new Swedish king of the new Swedish kingdom,
needed money for his treasury. Using theological ration-
ale modeled on the interpretation of the Bible imported
to Stockholm by the Swedish reformers who were Luther's
students, Vasa provided himself with the money in the
following way. Luther had written against monastic vows
in 1521. Only six years later radical economic consequences were drawn from it: monastic property and other
churchly riches were turned over to the Swedish crown.
It took a little longer for Vasa to establish armies, but
soon that political consequence of Luther's writings was
also drawn.[108] Pluralism thus ended in every country in
Europe, and strict orthodoxy was introduced and enforced
by law: Lutheranism in Scandinavia, Presbyterianism in
the Netherlands and Scotland, and Anglicanism in England.

A pluralism of "Christianities" emerged in Europe, but it
was a pluralism of churches that made war on each other
with sword in hand.

The directions of the fourth and of the sixteenth
century were thus antithetical. After Constantine, it was
considered good to break up small states. The peoples
were collected into the Empire and freed from their pro-
vincial limitations. After the Reformation it was considered good to encourage nation-states to flourish. The
individuality of the provinces was cultivated while pro-
hibitions were established against deviations. Yet at both
times the trend was unambiguous: going in a single direction. Furthermore, the same can be said concerning trends
in Europe in the twentieth century: it is clearly headed
in one direction, for the message of the churches is losing
its role and place in the legislation of the states.

There is no exception to this throughout Europe.
Laws of matrimony, divorce, abortion, and religious in-
struction are being consistently altered in our time in
such a way that the norms of the church are given a weaker
place in the law than has hitherto been the case—or they
are given no place at all. In no country is there a
strengthening of the functions of the church through established law. What the church still achieves with regard
to opinion-creating rests merely on the power of its word
and on the voluntary respect and esteem that it receives
from the citizens. In some countries the power and the
respect that follows from its word are considerable. Yet
the power of the church over people generally rests less
and less on the laws of the state, a radical change in
comparison to both the fourth and the sixteenth centuries.
It is necessary to acquire a broad perspective extending
over thousands of years if we are going to be able to

discover the contours of the change that is now taking place.

The merging of the church and state during the long period that has now drawn to its close meant that, almost in an unconscious way, the Christian message was communicated to the peoples of Europe. It is sufficient to mention only external traits of great importance, such as the ecclesiastical year and the phenomenon of the parish. Both function in the same remarkable way, for both allow the content of the Gospel to effect everyday news items of a trivial kind. "It was at Easter that year" we say when we try to recall an event; or we mention events in the life of Jesus, such as Christmas, Easter, and other festivals when we make our plans for the coming year. Moreover, the parish phenomenon—existing only in Europe— is still more remarkable. When someone is asked about the place of his birth, he mentions a place that is at the same time a congregation of baptized members in the primitive Christian sense. For more than a thousand years a "Christian congregation" referred to a "territory," albeit with people in it, but nonetheless primarily a territory with geographical boundaries.

This should not be looked at askance.[109] On the basis of the parish system in Europe a segregated church with separate black and white congregations could never arise. The question of which congregation an individual belonged to was decided by which street that person lived on. Race or skin color meant nothing. But at the same time, unfortunately, due to this external arrangement the preaching of the Gospel became unconscious, diffuse, and ambiguous. Moreover, the confession concerning the Creator, which also undoubtedly acquired an expression in the European parish system, and the confession of the unity of

God's work with us and the gifts of the earth round
about us became ambiguous and easy to forget. Platonizing
religion promoted this tendency, as in the Pietist and
in the Revivalist movements. If one were a pious Christian, one would sometimes flee from "social affairs" and
leave them to worldly persons. Furthermore, from the
mid-nineteenth century onward,this flight was facilitated
in most places in Europe by a division of most European
parishes into a civil and an ecclesiastical community.
Exactly such circumstances foreshadowed a coming break
of relations between church and state. The First Article
of the Creed (which concerns Creation) is the point in
the Trinitarian Confession first endangered by this kind
of break. And since everything in the Creed hangs together, the Gospel (or the Second Article) is also threatened, just as is the whole concept of the church (or the
Third Article). For example, institutional factors, foremost among which is the ministry, are beginning to become
primary in the church. These risks are now coming into
view with great clarity and can be seen in the formation
of proposals about the future relationship of church and
state that are now being presented in different European
countries.

The two different lines in European ecclesiastical
history after the Enlightenment that I have traced in a
previous section of this present work are appearing again.
We found two opposed lines that are both reductions of
the content of the Creed. On the one hand we confront a
bright and optimistic Creation faith without the idea of
destruction and the "devil," and without eschatology.
This theology starts out from the First Article of faith
and glosses over earthly human life and death with a
kindly brightness. On the other front a negative type

of Christianity is marshalling support. It is a negative,
Christocentric theology that draws sharp boundaries between church and world and that is at once militant and
evasive. Pietism, the Revivalist movements, Kierkegaard,
and Karl Barth belong here. Creation faith is weak in
this line. Indeed, sometimes even the term "Schöpfung"
or "Creation" is seen as a spiritual danger. By no means
have these two reduced types of theology died out today;
they still dominate the ecclesiastical arena in Europe.

On the whole we can characterize the responses of
these two groups to a future separation of church and
state in Europe in the following way: the less of a Christocentric, kerygmatic profile, the greater the aversion
to separation; and in the opposite direction, the less of
a classical living faith in the Creator, the greater the
desire to fortify the church and to separate it from the
state. Fundamentalists with an a-historical view of the
Bible, based on the theory of verbal inspiration; High
Church sacramentalists with an authoritative view of the
ministry; legalistic revivalist groups hastily deciding
who the "converted" and the "unconverted" are: such groups
unhesitantly desire the separation of church and state.
Groups which are offshoots from the bright and open optimism of the Enlightenment, made up of people with an
understanding of what God does among his creatures and in
the earthly realm, speak for maintaining a connection between state and church in the future. Seldom, however,
does this group have any feeling for the core of the
kerygma.

This is a serious situation in the ecclesiastical
history of Europe. For what will happen within a few
decades is quite clear: through measures from parliaments
and governments the church will actually be placed in a

radically new situation, separated from the administra-
tive apparatus of society, and bereft of the support of
general legislation, which it had previously enjoyed
throughout practically all of Europe. But when this
happens, the only group of Christians who will assent
to what happens and will be prepared to take over responsibility for the European church in the future will
be the narrow group that has no Creation faith.

It is my view that in this situation the Christian
church prior to A.D. 300 will acquire greater theological importance than it has ever had before.[110]   Before
A.D. 300 the church in Europe was a minority, and sometimes even a persecuted minority. In no place where the
church was then at work could it exercise any influence
over the laws that were in force for all inhabitants of
the country. The effect of the words and deeds of the
church functioned outside of legislation, but there was,
nonetheless, a strong effect. It was this church that
composed the Trinitarian Creed in which the idea of the
Creation of "the heavens and the earth" comes first and
the idea of "the resurrection of the body" last. In
those days the First Article of faith was fundamental
to the Church Fathers for an interpretation of all other
parts of the Creed. It was fundamental for Christology,
for the view of the role of the church among men, for
eschatology. In none of these areas did the primacy of
Creation faith become a shallow and optimistic blindness
to destruction. On the contrary, a realistic view of the
power of evil was obvious, albeit clothed in mythological attire.

If in this context one attends to Irenaeus, who
played a greater role in the composition of the Trinitarian Creed than any other person, one finds the fol-

lowing six points to be of greatest importance for a
church detached from state support in the twentieth century:

1. In the present time when Christians will again
be a group within a majority of people who do not believe
in Christ, it is important to recover the second century's positive and open view of the pagans outside of
the church. It is remarkable that a church that was persecuted could have such a dispassionate and rational
view of the growing Roman Empire as Christians of the
second century had. Every person, literally everyone,
is, according to this second century conviction, about
the continuous work of the Creator in the world, an instrument of God. Because he is an instrument, he cannot
demand to be worshipped. The first Christian church's
acceptance of society as good, even if it is governed by
non-Christians, is combined with an absolute rejection
of every form of emperor worship. This attitude is
worthy of imitation by the minority church of the twentieth century.

2. When Christians in the present live with a
feeling of cultural isolation, we must be cautious not
to be tempted by obscurantism in our view of the life of
Jesus, of salvation (which is mediated by the Gospel),
and of the relation between what is "human" and what is
"Christian." When a fairly isolated Christian group,
whose faith is not shared by the majority of people
around it, tries to give strength and stability to its
conviction, the temptation is great to stress things that
are "supernatural": a miraculously given Bible, a Jesus
who never despairs, not even on the cross, etc. Compared
to such modern religious attempts to "surpass" the Gospel,
the clear and calm speech of the second century about

what is human in Jesus and about what is human in salvation appears as a way of bearing witness to the Gospel
that we ought to imitate today. Jesus becomes the giver
of life by emptying himself of divinity.[112] To be "saved"
is thus to become truly human again.

3. Today when eschatological hope has been separated from earthly hopes for a better future for people,
it is important to recover from the second century a
more fluid boundaryline between earth and heaven. For
various reasons Christianity has declared heretical not
only the doctrine of the millenium as the book of Revelation describes it (Rev. 20:4f.), but also other ideas
of a future in which the will of God is realized gradual-
ly and by stages.[113] The polemic of the reformers
against the doctrine of purgatory has contributed to
making the eschatological future into an absolutely
otherworldly condition that is foreign to us. On this
point too the theology of the second century is more open
and more human than most later types of doctrine are. The
Church Fathers are worthy of imitation in their linking
up with an existing hope without thereby trivializing
hope and identifying it with a political utopia.

4. Today, when church communities tend to increase
their rigidity about different forms of faith and different orders for divine worship, it is important to regain
the simple and natural acceptance of multiplicity that
was characteristic of the second century. The struggle
over Easter is an excellent example of multiplicity that
Irenaeus recommended for continuance. Easter, therefore,
was celebrated at different times in different parts of
the church, at least until A.D. 325. However, after A.D.
325 Easter became a festival in the state, and the state
demanded uniformity. The church, which in a few decades

in Europe will have its connection with the state severed,
needs models to cultivate the art of enduring multiplicity without disunity. On this point too the pre-Constan-
tinian Christian congregation is a good pattern for
twentieth century Christendom.[114]

It may generally be said that the church before
A.D. 300 succeeded in keeping the two competing terms of
Creation and Gospel in balance. But it was not only a
question of balance, for balance presupposes that two
things in some sense stand over against one another. It
was rather the case that the two continued to give each
other mutual support. This internal coordination of
Creation and Gospel appears most clearly in the fifth
and the sixth points.

5. Today, when members of the Christian churches
have fairly uncritically accepted the western style of
life and considered nature as an inexhaustible resource
placed at the free and uninhibited disposal of mankind,
it is important to regain the idea of the unity of
man and nature that second century Christianity represents.[115] Through the Old Testament, in which man is
assumed to meet the Creator in God's gifts of water,
trees and shrubs, sun and other life-promoting realities
in our surroundings, the Christian church in all centuries should have been able to learn respect for nature.
That this has actually not happened is due to many factors. (Greek philosophy with its contempt for "matter"
has played no small role.) But one factor of importance
is undoubtedly also the cooperation of the church with
states and economic powers.[116] Second century Christian
theology, which is the oldest theology we have, is in a
way the most modern of all.

At this point it is especially clear that Creation

and Gospel go together and become one single power for
the salvation of all mankind. Christ is the true Man who
frees his congregation for a right use of the gifts of
Creation and who thereby——this lies in the most distant
eschatological future——puts an end to the groaning of
Creation beneath the heavy yoke of mankind. Creation and
Gospel are not opposed to each other; rather they support
one another.

6. Today, when the churches are inclined to establish a front of their own against their surroundings by
means of a special morality with special norms, it is important to regain emphasis on the resurrection, a unique
occasion for joy and an emphasis that characterized Christian preaching of the second century in matters great and
small. Three processes, three kinds of movement, in this
early period of European ecclesiastical history merged
into one process: the movement of the congregation out-
wards towards mankind (mission), the movement of the congregation in hope towards a future for all (eschatology),
and the patience and striving of the congregation to bear
the common burdens of mankind (*diaconia*). The boundaryline between the church and the pagan world is there, but
it resembles the difference between the art of healing on
the one hand, and the healed illness, on the other. I know
no epoch in the history of the church that has been marked
by such an unusual atmosphere of joy on the boundaryline
of the church as the years prior to A.D. 300.

The art of healing occasions joy, which is
not primarily the joy of the healer but mostly the joy of
those healed and saved from illness. The whole church
with all of its activities exists to bestow goodness and
life upon those who are outside of the church. The core
of the Gospel is the resurrection of Christ, and this

core is Creation, new and victorious Creation that over-
comes destruction and death.[117] Creation and Gospel do
not tend in different directions, and need therefore not,
as after the Enlightenment, be balanced off against one
another. Instead they support one another. Indeed, they
are one.

In the sixteenth century there was a similar relationship. The cause for joy occasioned by the Gospel
was that life had been given anew to those harassed by
the law. The important contrast was between forgiveness
and guilt, not between resurrection and death, as in the
second century. But fundamentally the two are the
same.[118] However, people in the twentieth century stand
psychologically closer to the heathen of the classical
period than to the slave under the law of the sixteenth
century, who was burdened with guilt because of severe
judgments emanating from an energetic confessional insti-
tion encompassing all the inhabitants of Europe.

This difference between the second and the sixteenth centuries is also related to the different church
and state situations that existed in these two periods.
In the second century the Christian church was a minority
without support from the legislation of the state and
without any role as the official guardian of morality.
Today the church has again become a minority. And because of this we are again being forced back to the
origins and wellsprings of the Christian faith.

FOOTNOTES

[1] Einar Billing, *Luthers lära om staten* (Uppsala, 1900).

[2] Gustaf Aulén published *Den kristna försoningstanken* in 1930 [English: *Christus Victor* (London, 1931)]. Anders Nygren published part II of *Den kristna kärlekstanken* in 1936 [English: *Agape and Eros* (London, 1939)].

[3] For Aulén see the interesting work by Gert Nilsson, *Återställd mänsklighet--gudomlig seger* (Lund, 1976).

[4] *Predikan* (Lund, 1949) appeared in English under the title *The Living Word* (Philadelphia, 1960). *Teologiens metodfråga* (Lund, 1954) appeared two years earlier under the title *Theology in Conflict* (Philadelphia, 1958). It should be noted that the English reading public did not get the books in the chronological order in which the Swedish readers got them.

[5] Nygren, *Filosofisk och kristen etik* (Stockholm, 1923) pp. 267-69. This very important book has never been translated into any non-Swedish language.

[6] Both books appeared in short intervals in English: Philadelphia, 1957 and 1959, under the titles *Luther on Vocation* and *Man and the Incarnation: A Study in the Biblical Theology of Irenaeus,* respectively.

[7] This holds to some extent for the two large works that I published in the beginning of the seventies, namaly *Växling och kontinuitet. Teologiska kriterier* (Lund, 1972), and *Credo. Den kristna tros- och livsåskådningen* (Lund, 1974). The latter book is intended to be a fairly complete dogmatics, useful at an academic level in the Scandinavian countries. Neither of these two books has been translated into English.

[8] I develop this further in a small book from the early seventies, namely *Luther frigiven* (Lund, 1970).

[9] See Oscar Cullman, *The Earliest Christian Confessions* (London, 1943), pp. 38 and 50-53.

[10] More explicitly argued in my book *Två testamentem och tre artiklar* (Stockholm, 1976).

[11]The two dogmatic books have been published in English translation, namely *Creation and Law* (Philadelphia, 1961), and *Gospel and Church* (Philadelphia, 1964). For reasons that I have already touched upon, however, the elements from Luther in these dogmatic works are somewhat stronger than those from Irenaeus. The contrary is the case with my later dogmatic exposition, *Trons artiklar* (Lund, 1968) and the previously mentioned book *Credo,* which two books are much more strongly determined by Irenaeus.

[12]See, for instance, Jürgen Moltmann, *Umkehr zur Zukunft* (München u. Hamburg, 1970), pp. 115-123.

[13]See *Credo,* p. 188f.

[14]Cf. *Man and the Incarnation,* pp. 26-38 and 113-32.

[15]Rudolf Bultmann, *Glauben und Verstehen* (Tübingen, 1933), p. 140. Also, Martin Heidegger, *Sein und Zeit* (Freiburg, 1927), p. 275.

[16]Of this unity see my *Theology in Conflict,* pp. 45-65 and 129-49.

[17]A whole section of my book *Man and the Incarnation* is devoted to "The Kingdom of the Son" in Irenaeus' view. Cf. especially pp. 181-92.

[18]See, for example, K. E. Løgstrup, *Opgør med Kierkegaard* (København, 1968), pp. 103f. Many other passages in Løgstrup's writings could be cited.

[19]The dogmatics was soon published in a second edition: *Skabelse og Genløsning* (København, 1955).

[20]See Ole Jensen, *Theologie zwischen Illusion und Restriktion. Analyse und Kritik der existenz-kritischen Theologie bei dem jungen Wilhelm Hermann und bei Rudolf Bultmann* (München, 1975), pp. 267-77.

[21]That an "emptiness" of this kind is the highest existing human purity depends on the nature of Adam's sin, according to Genesis and according to Irenaeus. The sin consists of wanting to assemble things that are more than human and to strive to be "like God" (Genesis 3:5). Because of this ambition human life is destroyed. See *Man and the Incarnation,* pp. 118-21 and 124-26.

[22]Concerning the different variants, see "Skapelse och evangelium. Ett problem i modern dansk teologi," *Svensk teologisk kvartalskrift*, 53 (1977), pp. 8-10. The journal will hereafter be referred to as *STK*.

[23]More of this in my contribution to the Festschrift for Ratschow: *Denkender Glaube* (Berlin and New York, 1976), pp. 250-58.

[24]Cf. *Credo*, pp. 27-32.

[25]The references here concern my Swedish text of 1942. When *Luthers lära om kallelsen* was translated into English several years later and eventually published under the title *Luther on Vocation*, the book was made as easy to read as possible, above all by cutting down the notes. In the English text neither Althaus nor Søe is mentioned. However, it is possible to trace the critique of Althaus. See *Luther on Vocation*, p. 78.

[26]Cf. the clarifying analysis of F. Gerald Downing, *Has Christianity a Revelation?* (London, 1964), pp. 263-90.

[27]Cf. Paul Althaus, *Die Christliche Wahrheit* (Gütersloh, 1947), pp. 21-94.

[28]See, for instance, *Luther on Vocation*, pp. 143-61 and 213-34, where many passages from Luther are cited. What is called "Regeneration" in the English translation should perhaps rather be called "New Creation." Luther's definition of creation is "continuously to make new" (Creare est semper novum facere).

[29]I have treated the Lutheran suppression of this perspective by means of many examples in *Luther frigiven*.

[30]See *Luther on Vocation*, p. 159.

[31]Within monastic piety there was a preference for imitation of the acts of the saints. Luther is sarcastic in his criticism of this piety. See *Luther on Vocation*, pp. 171-84.

[32]I have recently taken up this crucial question for Lutheranism in a small publication entitled *Rättfärdiggörelse av tro* (Stockholm, 1978).

[33]Cf. *Vaxling och kontinuitet*, p. 182.

[34]Cf. O. Jensen, *Ibid.*, pp. 267-77.

[35]For a more explicit statement of this, see
"Skapelse och evangelium," *STK,* pp. 4 and 7.

[36]Cf. Jensen, *Ibid.,* p. 237.

[37]In my book *The Flight from Creation* (Minneapolis,
1971), I have described the theological situation after
the end of World War II more elaborately.

[38]See *The Living Word,* p. 15.

[39]On Barth's various essays concerning Law and Gospel, see my article "Evangelium und Gesetz," in *Antwort:
Karl Barth zum siebzigsten Geburtstag* (Zürich, 1956),
pp. 310-22.

[40]See Christoph Gestrich, *Neuzeitliches Denken und
die Spaltung der dialektischen Theologie* (Tübingen, 1977),
pp. 11f. and 386.

[41]I discuss these differences between East and West
in *Credo,* p. 163.   The Eastern tradition shows great re-
semblances to Irenaeus and his view of the Spirit.

[42]A clarifying description of thought in the Eastern church is given in a Danish doctoral thesis of a few
years ago: Anna Maria Aagaard, *Helliganden sendt til
Verden* [literally, *The Holy Spirit sent into the World*
(Aarhus, 1973), pp. 260-73].

[43]Iwand was a vicar until 1945 and then immediately
became professor at Göttingen.   Before he was prohibited
from lecturing in 1935, he had been a *docent* at Königsberg
and professor at Riga.   During the 1950s Iwand occupied a
leading position in the German Evangelical Church.

[44]During my time as guest professor, a "disputation"
between Iwand and me was arranged on the subject "Zwischen
Barth und Luther."   This became a long discussion continued for two nights and listened to by a large audience,
with Ernst Wolf as the chairman.   See Hans Joachim Iwand,
Nachgelassene Werke III (München, 1966), pp. 399-405.

[45]The distance to Barth can also be observed in
Iwand's earlier writings.   An analysis of Barth's approach appears in a famous article in *Theologische Blätter*
of 1935: "Jenseits von Gesetz und Evangelium."   This article was reprinted in Iwand, *Um den rechten Glauben*
(München, 1959), pp. 87-109.

[46]Actually the two books were written in the reverse order: *Predikan* in 1949 and *Teologiens metodfråga* in 1954.

[47]As an example, see Nygren, *Urkristendom och reformation* (Lund, 1932), pp. 82-115.

[48]See Karl Barth, *Der Römerbrief* (Zürich, 1947), p. xxiv. (All the prefaces of earlier editions are reprinted there).

[49]See Bultmann, *Kerygma und Mythos* (Hamburg, 1952), pp. 203-7. Bultmann was by profession an exegete and only in later years did he work as a systematician.

[50]Cf. the exposition in *Växling och kontinuitet,* pp. 180-2.

[51]In Einar Billing this was a central point. For more about this, see my *An Exodus Theology, Einar Billing and the Development of Modern Swedish Theology* (Philadelphia, 1969).

[52]I present many passages from Barth's writings on this point in *Antwort,* pp. 311-19.

[53]Eberhard Amelung's article "Autonomie" in *Theologisches Realenzyklopädie IV* (Berlin, 1979) is very clarifying.

[54]This is the core of Jensen's attack on theology and the church during the last 200 years. See his *Theologie zwischen Illusion und Restriktion,* pp. 275-7.

[55]An explicit criticism of this view of Revelation appears in *Credo,* pp. 28-30.

[56]As early as the second century the Church Fathers repudiated "modalism," a heresy that identified God with Jesus and that isolated certain statements in the Gospel of John, as for instance John 14:9.

[57]See also "Skapelse och evangelium," *STK,* pp. 4-7.

[58]This concentration is also noticeable in the English edition. See the index with its many references to "Kerygma," "Law," and "Martin Luther" (*Theology in Conflict,* p. 170).

[59]There are suggestions in this direction in *Theology in Conflict,* pp. 81-2. I give more explicit analysis in *Credo,* pp. 58-62.

[60]Jesus' miracles of healing have such an effect of short duration. See *Credo,* pp. 79-92.

[61]In the English translation most of the footnotes are unfortunately omitted. For instance, two footnotes from *Predikan,* pp. 18 and 309, were eliminated.

[62]The text quoted from Luther is not an isolated one. Several similar statements are collected in Regin Prenter, *Spiritus Creator* (København, 1944), pp. 142 f.

[63]See the chapter on the "Sanctification of Time" in Gregory Dix, *The Shape of the Liturgy* (London, 1960).

[64]Of the consequences of this view for the interpretation of the Third Article of faith in its entirety, see *Credo,* pp. 143-89. The Spirit works in the external word, which, in every new situation, "distributes" the liberating actions of Christ.

[65]See also *Växling och kontinuitet,* pp. 46-9, and the small book, *Två testamenten och tre artiklar,* pp. 5-11. The latter is entirely devoted to the problem of the two testaments.

[66]The foremost contemporary theologian on the methodological level is Anders Jeffner, professor at Uppsala since 1976. See his *The Study of Religious Language* (London, 1972).

[67]Typical is the well written and already internationally known work by Birger Gerhardsson, *Memory and Manuscript. Oral Tradition and Written Transmission in Rabbinic Judaism and Early Christianity* (2nd. ed., Lund and Copenhagen, 1964). The High Church view of office might receive a certain support from these exegetical ideas ("tradition," "the beginning in Jesus himself and his choice of Apostles"). However, the High Church movement can find no support whatsoever in the kerygma about the death and resurrection of Jesus. From this point of view, too, it has been harmful that the kerygmatic approach has been lacking in Swedish theology.

[68]See especially *The Living Word,* p. 148, note 2 on the absence of the diaconate in Luther and on the

importance of the healing miracles of Jesus in the theology of the Church Fathers. It is Irenaeus who follows the New Testament here. Luther leaves the body to the realm of "the law" or "the secular regiment."

[69]Concerning this terminology, see *Theology in Conflict,* pp. viii-x.

[70]The beginning was with Ingemar Hedenius, *Tro och vetande* (Stockholm, 1949). The battle was then continued for almost two decades, especially by means of articles in the daily papers.

[71]Fridrichsen, Odeberg, and Riesenfeld in 1951 signed the so-called "exegetical declaration," in which it was asserted that the New Testament does not allow the ordination of women. In the Church Synod of 1958 Nygren expressed his theologically motivated reservation about the much disputed resolution adopted in 1958. To this day, Bishop Bo Giertz, the leader of the opposition to the ordination of women, cites these two documents.

[72]Friedrich Gogarten, *Verhängnis und Hoffnung der Neuzeit* (Stuttgart, 1953), p. 138.

[73]*Ibid.,* pp. 31-4. See also Gogarten's earlier work, *Die Kirche in der Welt* (Heidelberg, 1948), pp. 133 f.

[74]Einar Billing, who is unfortunately a relatively unknown theologian, continuously took up this point as the decisive conflict between biblical faith and Greek philosophy. See my *An Exodus Theology,* pp. 24-72.

[75]Only then will it truly be a question of freedom. It is the Gospel that gives freedom. The work of God through Creation and Law gives us work on earth. Cf. Jensen, *Ibid.,* pp. 277-85.

[76]See also my book *Luther frigiven,* pp. 79-89.

[77]See Jensen, *I vaekstens vold* (København, 1976), pp. 50-63. Personally, I am of the opinion that criticism should be directed against Gogarten on this point, for he is the pioneer.

[78]Gogarten, *Verhängnis und Hoffnung,* pp. 138 f.

[79]See also my article "Skapelse och evangelium," *STK,* p. 6f., especially the footnotes.

[80]This English text is a literal translation of my Swedish preface to *Skapelsen och lagen*. It is dated September, 1957 (p. 5 f.).

[81]Both books were published in Philadelphia. The unity between them was strongly indicated. See for instance also *Gosepl and Church*, p. v.

[82]It should be added here that both also exist in German translation with an equally strong indication of the unity: *Schöpfung und Gesetz* (Göttingen, 1960), and *Evangelium und Kirche* (Göttingen, 1963).

[83]See *Gospel and Church*, p. 5., especially note 4. See also *Credo*, pp. 56-74, where the exposition is more explicit.

[84]On the connection between the different statements in Romans 1-2, see C. A. Pierce, *Conscience in the New Testament* (London, 1955), p. 85 f.

[85]Cf. Daniel D. Williams, *The Spirit and the Forms of Love* (New York and Evanston, 1968), pp. 250-5.

[86]See my book *Luther on Vocation*, pp. 143-61. Regarding the sentence "Creare est semper novum facere," see especially p. 159 f.

[87]From the Catholic side, see the contribution by Bruno Schiller, "Katolsk moralteologi," in *Etik och kristen tro*, ed. G. Wingren (København, Oslo, Lund, 1971), pp. 104-6.

[88]Joachim Jeremias' analysis of the teaching of Jesus is of the greatest interest on this point. See his *Neutestamentliche Theologie* (Gütersloh, 1971), pp. 106 f. and 110-23.

[89]More explicitly in *Luther on Vocation*, pp. 61-3.

[90]If Dietrich Bonhoeffer had been an historian, he would have found good examples of "non-religious" speech about God in earlier periods.

[91]See Lars-Olle Armgard, *Antropologi. Problem i K. E. Løgstrup författarskap* (Lund and København, 1971); see also my article "Skapelse och evangelium," *STK*, pp. 1-11.

[92]Concerning the inner connection between these points, see *The Living Word*, pp. 137-63. Concerning demythologizing it should also be clearly said that the doctrine of the Virgin Birth is a part of the system of doctrines that could be dispensed of without loss. See *Credo*, pp. 79-82.

[93]See Løgstrup, *Skabelse og tilintetgorelse, Metafysik IV* (København, 1978), pp. 267-72. Cf. Armgard, *Ibid.*, pp. 210.

[94]See Løgstrup, *Kunst og etik* (København, 1961), pp. 233-5. An excellent analysis of this is given by Armgard, *Ibid.*, pp. 180-3.

[95]Cf. *Luther on Vocation*, p. 106.

[96]Cf. Løgstrup, *Skabelse og tilintetgorelse*, pp. 277-9. These pages in Løgstrup's latest book constitute a direct answer to my article "Skapelse och evangelium." Of course, there is profound significance in Løgstrup's choice of a title for this new volume: literally it means *Creation and Annihilation*.

[97]This is the main theme of my book *Credo*. See pp. 106 f., 114, 117-9, 174 f. and 184 f.

[98]Even for a much later exegesis the chapter by H. J. Holtzmann on the resurrection is typical. See his *Lehrbuch der neutestamentlichen Theologie* (Tübingen, 1911), pp. 427-33. For a criticism of this whole argument, see Per Frostin, *Politik och hermeneutik* (Lund, 1970), p. 159 f. Bultmann stands in the German Idealistic tradition.

[99]The great conflict with the state concerned the refusal to take part in the cult of the Emperor. See my contribution to the Nordic symposium in Uppsala of 1977: "Livsåskådningarna och frågan om kristendomens egenart," in *Livsåskådningsforskning* (Uppsala, 1977), pp. 197-9.

[100]Cf. Hans von Campenhausen, *Der Ablauf der Osterereignisse und das leere Grab* (Heidelberg, 1952), pp. 39-62.

[101]This is carried out in my popular exposition of the Trinitarian Creed, *Trons artiklar* (Lund, 1968).

[102]Latin American "Liberation Theology" is treated in a helpful way by Manfred Hofman in *Identifikation mit dem Anderen* (Stockholm and Göttingen, 1978).

[103]Cf. Paul Minear, *Christian Hope and the Second Coming of Christ* (Philadelphia, 1954), pp. 99-114.

[104]The relation between the sun and the sunbeam is a symbol which is used very early and which is also used in the formulation of the Second Article of the Nicene Creed. See Bengt Hägglund, *Teologins historia* (Lund, 1966), p. 38. Cf. *Credo*, p. 123.

[105]In 1972 a Swedish parliamentary commission presented a proposal about the separation of church and state, a proposal that I personally found well founded and reasonable. Hence the title of the book: *Svaret är ja* (Lund, 1972). Moreover, a great number of articles and contributions to this question have been published. I have done some alone and some in cooperation with others.

[106]About these theological theories in the fourth century, see Erik Peterson, *Frühkirche, Judentum und Gnosis* (Rome, 1959), pp. 51-9.

[107]This theme of the openness of the Gospel to multiplicity is a main theme in *Växling och kontinuitet*.

[108]When this consequence is drawn, Martin Luther's criticism of the medieval Crusades will have been long forgotten. According to Luther, faith can never be supported or expanded with weapons. See *Luther on Vocation*, pp. 107-15.

[109]The whole idea of church in Einar Billing is built on the geographical principle, which is "the clearest of all expressions of the Gospel." See also *An Exodus Theology*, pp. 90-102.

[110]After A.D. 300 the church left its minority status behind. After A.D. 1500 (the epoch of national churches) the church could not return to the situation before Constantine since the princes now began to use the confessionally determined national churches for their own state education of the people. Moreover, they did this with the help of a strict and homogenizing "Christian" legislation. Not until our time does a situation arise to which the theology of the Church

Fathers, which stresses the unity of Creation and Gospel, becomes fully relevant.

[111]See *Man and the Incarnation,* pp. 10-3.

[112]*Ibid.,* pp. 116-22.

[113]In the earlier forms of eschatological ideas a New Testament passage such as I Cor. 15:24-28 played quite a central role. See *Man and the Incarnation,* pp. 183-92.

[114]Concerning the Easter struggle and the mediating role played by Irenaeus, see *Man and the Incarnation,* p. 167.

[115]The exposition of the texts about "the cursing of the ground" and "the groaning of creation" is remarkable in its affinity to the ecological crisis we experience today (Genesis 3:17-19 and Romans 8:19-22). See *Man and the Incarnation,* p. 185 f., especially the whole section on "The Kingdom of the Son," pp. 181-92.

[116]Cf. Jensen, *Theologie,* pp. 236-42, 251, and 267-77, on the necessity of a new Old Testament science of exegesis.

[117]On this see *Man and the Incarnation,* p. 67 f. and pp. 160-3, where several biblical texts are given a very surprising interpretation.

[118]Concerning this reasoning about the boundaries between the church and mankind, see *Växling och kontinuitet,* pp. 153-6 and *Credo,* pp. 134-6.

INDEX

BIBLICAL PASSAGES

NAMES

THE WRITINGS OF GUSTAF WINGREN

by

HENRY VANDER GOOT

    The following bibliography is a complete bibliography of the works of Gustaf Wingren from 1936 to 1979. Wingren's works are arranged in chronological order by year. In addition, an asterisk appears in the left margin before the titles of Wingren's most important articles. Abbreviations used in the bibliography are the following: *STK* for *Svensk Teologisk Kvartalskrift, TL* for *Theologische Literaturzeitung,* and *SJT* for *Scottish Journal of Theology.*

1936

*   "Marcions kristendomstolkning," *STK*, 12, 318-38.

1938

1.   Review of *Theologie der Entscheidung,* by Eklund. *STK*, 14, 267-70.

2.   Review of *Erkend. og Virkeliggør af d. gode,* by Søe. *STK*, 14, 90-95.

1939

    "Ur tidskrifterna 1938," *STK*, 15, 99-104.

1940

1.   Review of *Förlåtelsetanken hos Luther och i nyare evangelisk teologi,* by von Engeström. *STK*, 16, 186-94.

2.   "Frälsningens Gud såsom skapare och domare," *STK,* 16, 322-39.

3.   "Skapelsen, lagen och inkarnationen enligt Irenaeus," *STK*, 16, 133-55.

1941

1.   Review of *Swedish Contributions to Modern Theology,* by Ferré. *STK*, 17, 241-48.

2.   Review of *Grundzüge der Theologie Luthers,* by Seeberg. *STK*, 17, 146-55.

3. Review of *Die Theologie Luthers,* by Walter. *STK,* 1?
    146-55.

1942

1. "Kyrkan och kallelsen." In *En bok om kyrkan.* Ed.
    G. Aulén. Stockholm, pp. 384-95. (German:
    "Kirche und Beruf." In *Ein Buch von der Kirche.*
    Göttingen: Vandenhoeck und Ruprecht, 1952, pp.
    423-35; English: "The Church and the Christian
    Vocation." In *This is the Church.* Philadelphia:
    Muhlenberg Press, 1952.)

2. *Luthers lära om kallelsen.* Lund: Gleerups; 2nd. ed
    1948; 3rd. ed., 1960. (German: *Luthers Lehre vom
    Beruf.* München: Christian Kaiser Verlag, 1952.
    English: *Luther on Vocation.* Philadelphia: Muhlen-
    berg Press, 1957; *The Christian's Calling.* Edin-
    burgh and London: Oliver and Boyd Ltd., 1958.)

3. "The Christian's Calling according to Luther,"
    The Augustana Quarterly, 21, 3-16.

1944

1. "Den kristne och arbetet," *Vår lösen,* 35, 186-95.

2. "Om Einar Billings teologi," *STK,* 20, 271-301.
    (English: "The Theology of Einar Billing," *The
    Lutheran Quarterly,* 2 [Nov. 1950], 396-414; cont.
    3 [Feb. 1951], 60-69.)

3. Review of *The Theology of Charles Gore,* by Ekström.
    STK, 20, 224-30.

4. Review of *Die Anfechtung bei Martin Luther,* by
    Bühler. *STK,* 20, 230-32.

1945

1. "Från den teologiska samtiden," *STK,* 21, 334-36.

2. Review of *Mater Ecclesia: An Inquiry into the Con-
    cept of the Church as Mother in Early Christianity,*
    by Plumpe. *STK,* 21, 131-33.

1947

1. "The Church and the Calling," *The Augustana
    Quarterly,* 26, 305-15.

2. "Arbetsglädje," *Tidskrift för Sv. sjuksköterskor,*
    14, 341-45. Rpt. in *Hälsa och Själ.* Ed. Hillbom

and Nilsson. Stockholm: Sv. kristliges
studentrölrelse Bokförlag, pp. 198-211.

3. "Das Evangelium und die Mission," *Evangelische
    Missionsmagazin*, 91, 140-48. Cf. 1949, no. 2
    for Swedish.

*   4. "Geistliches und Weltliches Regiment bei Luther,"
        Theologische Zeitschrift, 3, 263-73.

*   5. "Gott und Mensch bei Karl Barth," *Studia Theo-
        logica*, 1, 27-53. Rpt. separately in the series
        Luthertum, Heft 2. Ed. J. Pfeiffer and H.
        Schlyter. Berlin: Lutherisches Verlagshaus, 1951.

6. *Människan och inkarnationen enligt Irenaeus.*
    Lund: Gleerups. (English: *Man and the Incarna-
    tion: A Study in the Biblical Theology of Irenaeus.*
    Philadelphia: Muhlenberg Press; Edinburgh and
    London: Oliver and Boyd Ltd., 1959.)

1948
1. Review of *Person och gemenskap*, by Johannesson.
    STK, 24, 44-58.

2. "'Ordet' hos Barth," *STK*, 24, 249-67. (English:
    "The Word of God in the Theology of Barth," *The
    London Quarterly and Holborn Review*, 1949, pp.
    333-46; cont. in 1950, pp. 50-56. Cf. *The Evan-
    gelical Quarterly*, 21 [Oct. 1949], 265-85. These
    two English manuscripts are independent transla-
    tions and, therefore, differ slightly.)

1949
1. "Arbetets mening," *STK*, 25, 278-86. (German:
    "Der Sinn der Arbeit," *Evangelische Theologie*,
    10 [1950/51], 39-48.)

2. "Evangeliet och missionen," *Den evangeliska
    missionen*, 103, 177-83. (Cf. 1947, 3. for German.)

3. *Predikan. En principiell studie.* Lund: Gleerups;
    2nd. ed., 1960. (German: *Die Predigt.* Berlin:
    Evangelische Verlagsanstalt, 1955; 2nd. ed.,
    Göttingen: Vandenhoeck und Ruprecht, 1959. Eng-
    lish: *The Living Word.* Philadelphia: Fortress
    Press, 1965.)

4. "The Word of God in the Theology of Barth," *The

London Quarterly and Holborn Review, 1949, pp.
333-46; cont. in 1950, pp. 50-56.   Cf. 1948, 2.

*   5.   "'Weg,' 'Wandrung,' und verwandte Begriffe,"
           Studia Theologica, 3, 111-23.

       6.   Review of Neue Studien zur lateinischen Irenaeus
           Übersetzung, by Lundström. STK, 25, 244-45.

1950
*   1.   "Tro och sanning," STK, 26, 7-23.

*   2.   Utläggningens problematik," STK, 26, 403-12.

       3.   "Femtio års religiös utveckling i Sverige."   In
           Seklets män 1900-50. Göteborg: Bokförlaget
           Antiqua, 1950, pp. 48-55.

*   4.   "Was bedeutet die Forderung der Nachfolge Christi
           in evangelischer Ethik?," TL 75 (July 1950), 386-
           91.

       5.   "Der Sinn der Arbeit," Evangelische Theologie,
           10 (1950/51), 39-48. Cf. 1949, 1.

       6.   "The Theology of Einar Billing," The Lutheran
           Quarterly, 2 (Nov. 1950), 396-413; cont. in 3
           (Feb. 1951), 60-69. Cf. 1944, 3.

1951
       1.   "Der Tod und des ewige Leben," Evangelische-
           lutherische Kirchenzeitung, 5, 325-27.

*   2.   "Några karakteristiska drag i modern teologi,"
           STK, 27, 241-47.

       3.   "Problematiken kring 1954 års världskyrkokonferens,
           Kristen gemenskap, 24, 172-75.

       4.   "Kirche und Beruf."   In Ein Buch von der Kirche.
           Ed. G. Aulen. Göttingen: Vandenhoeck und
           Ruprecht, 1951, pp. 423-35. Cf. 1942, 1.

1952
       1.   "Nya översiktsarbeten i teologisk etik" (Review
           of Die kirchliche Dogmatik III, 4, by Karl Barth;
           Christentum und Gemeinschaft, by Bennett; Das
           christliche Ethos, by Elert; Basic Christian
           Ethics, by Ramsey; and Theologische Ethik I, by

Thielicke.), *STK*, 28, 204-21.

2.   "Evangeliet i världen," *Vår lösen*, 43, 284-93.

3.   *Luthers Lehre vom Beruf*. München: Christian
     Kaiser Verlag. Cf. 1942, 2.

4.   "The Church and the Christian Vocation." In *This
     is the Church*. Ed. G. Aulén. Philadelphia:
     Muhlenberg Press. Cf. 1942, 1.

5.   "Vi och samhället," *Ny kyrklig Tidskrift*, 21,
     77-90. Rpt. as *Kyrkan och samhället*. Sveriges
     Kyrkliga Studentförbund Skriftserie. Stockholm:
     Studiebok Förlaget, 1958.

6.   "Förberedelser för Evanston," *STK*, 28, 297-98.

7.   "Ett nytt steg mot Evanston," *Kristen gemenskap*,
     25, 156-59.

1953
1.   "Arbejdets mål og mening," *Dansk Teologisk Tids-
     skrift*, 16, 28-36.

2.   "Den teologiska debatten inför Evanston," *Kristen
     gemenskap*, 26, 113-20.

3.   "Luthersk teologi och världsmissionen," *Svensk
     Missionstidskrift*, 41, 15-21. (German: "Luther-
     ische Theologie und Weltmission." In *Offizieller
     Bericht der 2 vollvers. des lutherischen Weltbundes*.
     Gumzenhausen, 1953.)

4.   "Det teologiska arbetet inon World Council," *STK*,
     29, 301-03.

5.   Review of *R. Bultmann: Ein Versuch ihn zu verstehen*,
     by Karl Barth. *STK*, 29, 42-52.

6.   Review of *Den korsfäste Skaparen*, by Bohin. *STK*,
     29, 163-65.

1954
1.   "Eschatological Hope and Social Action: the Ten-
     sion between European and American Theology,"
     Lutheran World, 1, 18-29.

2.   "Evanston," *STK*, 30, 246-61.

3.   *Toelogiens metodfråga*. Lund: Gleerups. (German:

Die Methodenfrage der Theologie. Göttingen:
Vandenhoeck und Ruprecht, 1957. English: *Theol-
ogy in Conflict.* Philadelphia: Muhlenberg Press;
Edinburgh and London: Oliver and Boyd Ltd., 1958.)

4. "Kristus--vårt hopp," *Vår lösen,* 45, 182-90.

5. "Bibeln och den mänskliga rättigheterna," *Vår
   lösen,* 45, 81-83.

6. Review of *Grundriss der Ethik,* by Althaus. *STK,*
   30, 198-99.

7. Review of *Verhängnis und Hoffnung der Neuzeit,* by
   Gogarten. *STK,* 30, 141-43.

1955

1. *Die Predigt.* Berlin: Evangelische Verlagsanstalt;
   2nd. ed., Göttingen: Vandenhoeck und Ruprecht,
   1959. Cf. 1949, 3.

2. "Einar Billings teologiska metod." In *Nordisk
   teologi. Till Ragnar Bring.* Lund: Gleerups, pp.
   279-92.

3. "En lång ekumenisk sommar. Kring aktuella Faith
   and Order problem," *Kristen gemenskap,* 28, 187-90.

4. "Kyrkans isolering," *Vår lösen,* 46, 355-58. Rpt.
   separately in Kyrkliga reformfrågor serie, No. 3.
   Stockholm: Sveriges Kristliga Studentrörelses
   Bokförlag, 1958. Cf. 1958, 4.

1956

1. "Arbetets mening ur teologisk synpunkt," *Vår
   lösen,* 47, 171-76.

* 2. "Evangelium und Gesetz." In *Antwort: Karl Barth
     zum siebzigsten Geburtstag.* Zürich: Evangelisches
     Verlag AG, pp. 310-22. Rpt. in *Gesetz und Evan-
     gelium.* Ed. E. Kinder and K. Haendler. Darmstadt:
     Wissenschaftliche Buchgesellschaft, 1968, pp. 260-
     276.

* 3. "Filosofi och teologi hos biskop Nygren," *STK,*
     32, 284-312.

* 4. "Nomos och agape hos biskop Nygren," *STK,* 32,
     122-32.

*   5.   "Teologiens metodfråga," STK, 32, 36-41.

*   6.   "Justification by Faith in Protestant Thought,"
            SJT, 9, 374-83.

*   7.   "Swedish Theology since 1900," SJT, 9, 133-34.
            Cf. 1958, 11.

       8.   "Sakkunigutlåtande rörande lediga professorämbetet
            i systematisk teologi vid Oslo universitet den 2.
            April 1953." In Universitet Oslo. Arsberetning
            1952-1953.

1957
       1.   Die Methodenfrage der Theologie. Göttingen:
            Vandenhoeck und Ruprecht. Cf. 1954, 3.

       2.   Luther on Vocation. Trans. Carl C. Rasmussen.
            Philadelphia: Muhlenberg Press. Cf. 1942, 2.

       3.   "Welt und Kirche unter Christus, dem Herrn,"
            Kerygma und Dogma, 3, 53-60. Rpt. in Reich
            Gottes und Welt: Die Lehre Luthers von den zwei
            Reichen. Ed. H.-H. Schrey. Darmstadt: Wissen-
            schaftliche Buchgesellschaft, 1969, pp. 339-49.

1958
       1.   "Die Sakramente und die Predigt als Träger des
            fleisch gewordenen Wortes," In:die Leibhaftigkeit
            des Wortes: Festschrift für Adolf Koberle zum
            sechigsten Geburtstag. Hamburg: IM Furche-Verlag,
            pp. 375-86.

       2.   "Ekumenik och teologi." In Studier tillägn. H.
            Lindroth. Uppsala: Lundequistska Bokhandeln, pp.
            140-50.

       3.   Kyrkan och samhället. Sveriges Kyrkliga Student-
            förbund Schriftserie. Stockholm: Studiebok
            Förlaget. Cf. 1952, 5.

       4.   Kyrkans isolering. Kyrkliga reformfragor serie,
            No. 3. Stockholm: Sveriges Kristliga Student-
            rörelses Bokförlag. Cf. 1955, 4.

       5.   Kyrkans ämbete. Ordet och Kyrkan serie. Lund:
            Gleerups.

       6.   "Svenska kyrkan och frikyrkorna," Vår lösen, 49,

179-85. Rpt. in *Kristet forum* (Oct. 7, 1958), pp. 17-23.

7. "Das dreigliedrige Glaubensbekenntnis," *Kerygma und Dogma*, 4, 66-72.

8. "Kyrkordning och enhet," *STK*, 34, 270-80. (English: "Church Order and Unity," *The Church Quarterly Review* [Jan.-March 1960], pp. 44-54.)

9. *Skapelsen och lagen*. Lund: Gleerups. (German: *Schöpfung und Gesetz*. Göttingen: Vandenhoeck und Ruprecht, 1960. English: *Creation and Law*. Philadelphia: Muhlenberg Press; Edinburgh and London: Oliver and Boyd Ltd., 1961.)

10. *Theology in Conflict*. Trans. Eric H. Wahlstrom. Philadelphia: Muhlenberg Press; Edinburgh and London: Oliver and Boyd Ltd. Cf. 1954, 3.

11. *Svensk teologi efter 1900*. Stockholm: Sveriges kristl. studentrörelse. Cf. 1956, 7.

1959

1. "Kyrka och folk," *Ny kyrklig Tidskrift*, 28, 1-12.

2. *Man and the Incarnation. A Study in the Biblical Theology of Irenaeus*. Trans. Ross Mackenzie. Philadelphia: Muhlenberg Press; Edinburgh and London: Oliver and Boyd Ltd. Cf. 1947, 6.

3. *Svenska kyrkans ekumeniska ansvar*. Ordet och Kyrkan serie. Lund: Gleerups.

4. "Vad betyder folkkyrkan? Om Einar Billing," *Vår lösen*, 50, 5-9.

1960

1. "Church Order and Unity," *The Church Quarterly Review* (Jan.-March), pp. 44-54. Cf. 1958, 8.

2. "Den teologiska etiken just nu," *Kyrkobröderna*, 1, 6-11.

3. "Läroauktoriteten i vår lutherska kyrka." In *Åpen kirke*. Oslo, pp. 104-15. (German: "Kritische Erwägungen zum Begriff der Lehrautorität in der lutherischen Kirche," *Kerygma und Dogma*, 10 [1964], 246-56.)

4. *Schöpfung und Gesetz*. Göttingen: Vandenhoeck und Ruprecht. Cf. 1958, 9.

5. *Evangeliet och kyrkan*. Lund: Gleerups. (German: *Evangelium und Kirche*. Göttingen: Vandenhoeck und Ruprecht, 1963. English: *Gospel and Church*. Philadelphia: Fortress Press; Edinburgh and London: Oliver and Boyd Ltd., 1964.)

6. *The Living Word: A Theological Study of Preaching and the Church*. Trans. Victor C. Pogue. Philadelphia: Muhlenberg Press; 2nd. ed., Fortress Press, 1965. Cf. 1949, 3.

7. "Det teologiska arbetet inom Faith and Order," *Kristen gemenskap*, 33, 114-30.

1961

1. *Creation and Law*. Trans. Ross Mackenzie. Philadelphia: Muhlenberg Press; Edinburgh and London: Oliver and Boyd Ltd. Cf. 1958, 9.

2. "Adam, Wir und Christus," *Kerygma und Dogma*, 7, 54-68.

3. "Den 'religiöst motiverade' folkkyrkan och den 'demokratiska' folkviljan," *Vår lösen*, 52, 188-92.

1963

1. *Evangelium und Kirche*. Göttingen: Vandenhoeck und Ruprecht. Cf. 1960, 5.

* 2. "Lag och evangeliet och deras konsekvenser för liv och gudsjänst," *Ny kyrklig Tidskrift*, 32, 163-76. (English: "Law and Gospel and their Implications for Christian Life and Worship," *Studia Theologica*, 17, 77-89.)

3. *Demokrati i folkkyrkan*. Ordet och Kyrkan serie. Lund: Gleerups.

* 4. "Gamla testamentets teologiska betydelse," *Ny kyrlig Tidskrift*, 32, 104-15.

5. "Neutralitet i religionsfrågor-en samhällsattityd under debatt," *Kristet forum*, 10, 150-52.

6. "Ordet och gärningarna," *Nordisk Missionstidskrift*, 74, 3-12.

1964

1. *Folkkyrkotanken.* Kyrkan i 60-talet serie.
    Stockholm: Diakonistyrelsen's Bokförlag.

2. *Gospel and Church.* Trans. Ross Mackenzie.
    Philadelphia: Fortress Press; Edinburgh and Lon-
    don: Oliver and Boyd Ltd. Cf. 1960, 5.

* 3. "The Main Lines of Development in Systematic
    Theology and Biblical Interpretation in Scandi-
    navia." Fifth Annual Bibliographical Lecture.
    The Library of Union Theological Seminary,
    Richmond, Virginia.

4. "Kritische Erwägungen zum Begriff der Lehrautorität
    in der lutherischen Kirche," *Kerygma und Dogma,*
    10, 246-56. Cf. 1960, 3.

5. "Nya internationella studieprojekt. Sammanträden
    i Pullach (LVF) och i Aarhus (FandO) sommaren
    1964," *Kristen gemenskap,* 37, 176-80.

6. "Utan ränsel, utan penningung." In *Samfund i
    Själyprövning.* By Gustaf Wingren, et al. Stock-
    holm: Gummesson's Bokförlag, pp. 25-32.

1965

1. "Gustaf Aulén." In *A Handbook of Christian Theo-
    logians.* Ed. D. G. Peerman and M. Marty. Cleve-
    land and New York: The World Publishing Company,
    pp. 308-19.

2. "Authority." In *The Encyclopedia of the Lutheran
    Church.* Ed. J. Bodensieck. Minneapolis, Minn.:
    Augsburg Publishing House, 1965, pp. 160-62.

1966

1. "Genom tron." Ystad: Bjurström and Co. Boktrycheri

2. "Mina ämnesval. Apologia pro vita mea. Teologiskt
    självporträtt," *Vår lösen,* 57, 494-500. (English:
    "Creation: A Crucial Article of Faith: My Selection
    of Topics," *Flight from Creation.* Minneapolis,
    Minn.: Augsburg Publishing House, 1971, pp. 13-30.)

1967

1. "Fram mot en enad kyrka," *Tro och liv,* 1, 3-10.

2. "Religionsfrihetslagen efter 15 år," *Svensk*

Tidskrift, 54, 7-16.

3. "Das Problem des Natürlichen bei Luther." In *Kirche, Mystik, Heilung und das Natürliche bei Luther.* Göttingen: Vandenhoeck und Ruprecht, pp. 156-68. (Swedish: "Det naturligas problem hos Luther," *Luther frigiven.* Lund: Gleerups, 1970, pp. 9-25. Cf. 1970, 2.)

* 4. "Vad betyder Luther i day?." In *Luther i dag. Svenska kyrkans reformations jubileum.* Lund: Håkan Ohlssons Förlag, pp. 5-26. Rpt. in *Luther frigiven.* Lund: Gleerups, 1970, pp. 43-63. Cf. 1970, 2.

* 5. "Reform and Reformation. Two Perspectives," *Lutheran World,* 14, 345-50. (German: "Reform und Reformation," Lutherische Rundschau, 17 [Oct. 1967], 445-51.)

6. "Skapelsen--en ny problematik i Faith and Order." In *Festskrift til Regin Prenter.* København: Gyldendals Boghandel. Nordisk Forlag, pp. 118-24.

1968

1. *Einar Billing. En studie i svensk teologi före 1920.* Lund: Gleerups. (German: *Gestalt einer Kirche von Morgen: Der Theologische Entwurf des Schweden Einar Billing.* München: Verlag Claudius, 1969. English: *An Exodus Theology: Einar Billing and the Development of Modern Swedish Theology.* Philadelphia: Fortress Press, 1969.)

2. "Kallelsetanken. Grundvalar och problem," *Årsbok för kristen humanism 1968,* 30, 58-68. Rpt. in *Luther frigiven.* Lund: Gleerups, 1970, pp. 64-78. Cf. 1970, 2. (German: "Der Begriff des Berufs-- Grundlage und Probleme," *Lutherische Rundschau,* 18 [1968], 103-14. English: "The Concept of Vo- cation--Its Basis and Problems," *Lutheran World,* 15 [1968], 87-95.)

* 3. "Der Meister und seine Jünger," *TL,* 93, 81-86.

* 4. *Trons artiklar.* Lund: Gleerups. (German: *Adam sind Wir. Drei Vorträge zum Glaubensbekenntnis.* München: Claudius Verlag, 1970.)

* 5. "Reformation und Weltlichkeit." In *Reformation*

1517-1967. *Wittenberger Vorträge.* Ed. E. Kähler.
Berlin: Evangelische Verlag, pp. 20-27. (Swedish:
"Skapelsetro och sekularis eringsteologi," *Arsbok
för kristen humanism 1968.* Rpt. in *Luther frigiven*
Lund: Gleerups, 1970, pp. 79-89.)

6. "Kristologi och antropologi i vår tid. Evangelium
    nu." In *Tolkning. Teologer samtalar.* Ed. Olov
    Hartman. Stockholm: Verbum/Kyrkliga Central-
    förlaget, pp. 77-89.

1969

1. *An Exodus Theology: Einar Billing and the Develop-
    ment of Modern Swedish Theology.* Trans. Eric
    Wahlstrom. Philadelphia: Fortress Press. Cf. 1968,
    1.

2. *Gestalt einer Kirche von Morgen. Der Theologische
    Entwurf des Schweden Einar Billing.* München:
    Verlag Claudius. Cf. 1968, 1.

3. "Den lutherska synen på äktenskapet." In *I fråga
    satt.* Ed. Monica Boethius. Stockholm: Verbum.
    Rpt. in *Luther frigiven.* Lund: Gleerups, 1970,
    pp. 26-42.

*   4. "Från ordningsteologi till revolutionsteologi,"
        STK, 45, 37-47. (German: "Von der Ordnungsthe-
        ologie zur Revolutionstheologie," *Neue Zeitschrift
        für Systematische Theologie und Religionsphiloso-
        phie,* 12 [1970], 1-12. English: "Creation and
        Ethics. From Ordnungstheologie to the Theology
        of Revolution," *Flight from Creation.* Minneapolis:
        Augsburg Press, 1971, pp. 33-53.)

5. "Ein ungenutztes ökumenisches Kapital," *Evangelisch
    Kommentare,* 2, 701-06. (Swedish: "Augustana VII
    och dagens ekumenik," *STK,* 46 [1970], 1-16.)

6. "Alla," *Svensk Missionstidskrift,* 3, 117-22.

7. "Den klassiska lutherdoms ethos," *Lumen,* 12, 73-
    80. Rpt. in *Luther frigiven.* Lund: Gleerups,
    1970, pp. 90-101.

8. "Hur kan etiska värden påverka teknisk utveckling?,
    Var lösen, 60, 535-37.

1970

*   1. *Adam sind Wir. Drei Vorträge zum Glaubensbekenntnis.*

München: Claudius Verlag. Cf. 1968, 4.

*   2.   *Luther frigiven.* Lund: Gleerups. Cf. 1967, 3
          and 4; 1968, 2 and 5; and 1969, 3 and 7.

     3.   "Mer än enhet mellan kyrkorna," *Vår lösen,* 61,
          419-23.

     4.   "Augustana VII och dagens ekumenik," *STK,* 46, 1-
          16. Cf. 1969, 5.

*   5.   "Von der Ordnungstheologie zur Revolutions-
          theologie," *Neue Zeitschrift für Systematische
          Theologie und Religionsphilosophie,* 12, 1-12.
          Cf. 1969, 4.

*   6.   "Theologie zwischen Dogmatik und Analyse," *Neue
          Zeitschrift für Systematische Theologie und
          Religionsphilosophie,* 12, 184-95. (English:
          "Creation and Theology: Theology between Dogmatics
          and Analysis," *Flight from Creation.* Minneapolis:
          Augsburg Press, 1971, pp. 57-76.)

*   7.   "Martin Luther in zwei Funktionen." In *Rheinisch-
          Westfälische Akademie der Wissenschaften.
          Vorträge G 168.* Opladen: Westdeutscher Verlag,
          pp. 7-27.

     8.   *Socialetik i Stockholm.* Uppsala: Bokförlaget Pro
          Veritate.

1971
*   1.   *Flight from Creation.* Minneapolis: Augsburg Press.
          Cf. 1966, 2; 1969, 4; and 1970, 5 and 6.

     2.   "Ausserhalb unserer selbst oder woran uns Luther
          erinnert." In *Zur Sache.* Ed. S. von Kortzfleisch.
          Hamburg: Lutherischer Verlagshaus, pp. 21-28.

     3.   "Förkunnelsen av evangeliet i vår tid." *Tro och
          liv,* 3, 98-106.

     4.   "Vårt behov av makt," *Vår lösen,* 62, 96-97.

     5.   *Fram emot en enad kyrka. Variationen över Matt.
          28:18-20.* Stockholm: Gummessons.

     6.   "Reformationens och lutherdomens ethos." In *Etik
          och kristen tro.* Ed. G. Wingren. Lund: Gleerups;

København: Gyldendal; Oslo: Universitets forlaget,
pp. 112-47.

1972

1. *Växling och kontinuitet. Teologiska kriterier.*
Lund: Gleerups.

2. *Svaret är ja. Ett ord om kyrka och stat.* Lund:
Gleerups.

3. "Värderingar inom den systematiska teologin," *STK*,
48, 25-33.

* 4. "Was geschah eigentlich in Lund in den dreissiger
Jahren?," *TL*, 97, 885-90.

5. "Dogmatikern Ige Lønning," *Nordisk Teologisk
Tidskrift*, 73, 217-25.

6. "Vad kan vi komma att få från svensk högkyrklighet
i framtiden?" In *Opuscula Ecclesiastica. Studier
tillagnäde Gunnar Rosendal*. Uppsala: Bokförlaget
Pro Veritate, pp. 426-33.

7. "Kyrkans människosyn," *Årsbok för kristen humanism
1972*, 34, 30-43.

1973

"Jesus i kyrkorna och i världen." In *Jesus aterupp-
täckt?* Ed. Vargit Sahlin. Stockholm: Albert Bonniers
Förlag AB, pp. 140-50.

1974

* 1. "Den springande punkten," *STK*, 3, 101-07.

2. *Credo. Den kristna tros- och livsåskådningen.*
Lund: Gleerups.

3. *Maria. Ett ord om människovård.* Lund: Håkan
Ohlssons.

4. "Alla folk," *Vår lösen*, 65, 330-33.

5. "Kristendom och marxism om det onda," *Kristet
forum*, 8-9, 8-12.

* 6. "Die Welt Gottes und der Einzelne." In *Evangelium
als Geschichte*. Ed. V. Vajta. Göttingen: Vandenhoeck und Ruprecht, pp. 52-85. (English: "God's

World and the Individual." In *The Gospel as History*. Ed. V. Vajta. Philadelphia: Fortress Press, 1975, pp. 43-75.)

7. "Irenaeus, Saint," *Encyclopedia Britannica*. 15th ed. USA: Helen Hemingway Benton, 9, 889-890.

1975

1. *"I beygnnelsen skapade Gud..." Sex radioandakter om skapelsen.* Falköping: Gummessons Boktryckeri AB.

* 2. "God's World and the Individual." In *The Gospel as History*. Ed. V. Vajta. Philadelphia: Fortress Press, pp. 43-75. Cf. 1974, 6.

3. "Kyrkans samhällsansvar," *Kirke og Kultur,* pp. 129-40.

4. "Human Rights: A Theological Analysis," *The Ecumenical Review,* pp. 124-27.

5. "De tre skovlarna, arken och giftbägaren," *Vår lösen,* 6, 327-29.

6. "Byggnaderna eller funktionen?," *Vår lösen,* 6, 356-64.

7. "Kristen och human socialetik." In *Kyrkans samhällsansvar.* Ed. Carl-Henric Grenholm. Stockholm: Verbum, pp. 71-94.

8. *Frigörelse till livskvalitet.* Stockholm: Gummessons.

1976 1. "Lars Ahlin = Evangelium = Obegriplighet." In *Årsbok 1975 för Föreningen Lärare i Religionskunskap.* Klippan: Ljungbergs boktryckeri, pp. 74-77.

2. "Långfredagens och påskdagens texter." *Tro och liv,* pp. 15-21.

3. "Heil und Wohl des Menschen in biblischer und aktueller Sicht." In *Denkender Glaube. Festschrift - - - Carl Heinz Ratschow - - -.* Ed. Otto Kaiser. Berlin: Walter de Gruyter, pp. 250-8.

4. *Två testamenten och tre artiklar.* Stockholm:

Gummessons.

5. "En kristen människosyn." In Årsbok för Kristen
    Humanism, 38.   Ed. Carl Henric Grenholm.   Stock-
    holm: Gummessons, pp. 11-23.

6. "Fragen um das Personsein Gottes." Theologische
    Literaturzeitung, 101, pp. 722-8.

1977
1. "Das Abendmahl als Tischgemeinschaft nach
    ethischen Gesichtspunkten." In Theologische
    Realencyklopädie I. Berlin: Walter de Gruyter,
    pp. 212-29.

2. "Skapelse och evangelium.   Ett problem i modern
    dansk teologi." STK, pp. 1-11.

3. ...en framtid och ett hopp.   Fyra morgonandakter.
    Stockholm: Verbum.

4. "Livsåskådningarna och frågan om kristendomens
    egenart." In Acta Universitatis Upsaliensis:
    Symposia Universitatis Upsaliensis Annum
    Quingentesimum Celebrantis 4: Livsåskådnings-
    forskning.   Stockholm: Almqvist & Wiksell Inter-
    national, pp. 183-203.

5. "Är trons gemenskap en förutsättning för
    gudstjänsten eller skapar gudstjänsten trons
    gemenskap?"   In Gudstjenesten og hverdagen.
    Konferens om gudstjänstförnyelse i Helsingör.
    Sigtuna: Nordiska ekumeniska institutet, pp. 37-
    44.

1978
1. "Storasyster hjälper mamma." Tro och liv, pp.
    8-12.

2. "Efter 1984." In En levande kyrka.   Ed. Kjell
    Ove Nilsson.   Stockholm: Verbum, pp. 17-27.

3. Rättfärdiggörelse av tro. Fem lutherska morgonböner.
    Stockholm: Verbum.

4. "Människan som skapelse och som produkt."
    Praesteforeningens Blad (Copenhagen), pp. 593-
    604.

5. "Konfrontation med lagen." In Kamp och lovsång.